# *WORKBOOK*

to accompany

# Psychology

## and You

**Third Edition**

*Prepared by*

## Barbara G. Wiggins

West Educational Publishing

*an International Thomson Publishing company* I(T)P®

Cincinnati ◆ Albany, NY ◆ Belmont, CA ◆ Bonn ◆ Boston ◆ Detroit ◆ Johannesburg ◆ London ◆ Los Angeles
Madrid ◆ Melbourne ◆ Mexico City ◆ New York ◆ Paris ◆ Singapore ◆ Tokyo ◆ Toronto ◆ Washington

COPYRIGHT © 2000    By WEST EDUCATIONAL PUBLISHING
An International Thomson Publishing company
ɪⓉᴘ    The ITP logo is a trademark under license.

4  5  6  7  8    021    07  06  05

ISBN  0-538-42663-2

# Contents

**Chapter 1: THE FIELD OF PSYCHOLOGY**

Vocabulary . . . . . . . . . . . . . . . . . . . . . . . . . . . . . . . . . . . . . . . . . . . . . . . . . . .1-1
Review/Test Preparation . . . . . . . . . . . . . . . . . . . . . . . . . . . . . . . . . . . . . .1-2
Worksheet . . . . . . . . . . . . . . . . . . . . . . . . . . . . . . . . . . . . . . . . . . . . . . . . . . .1-5
Discussion . . . . . . . . . . . . . . . . . . . . . . . . . . . . . . . . . . . . . . . . . . . . . . . . . . .1-6
Activities . . . . . . . . . . . . . . . . . . . . . . . . . . . . . . . . . . . . . . . . . . . . . . . . . . . .1-7

**Chapter 2: METHODS OF PSYCHOLOGY**

Vocabulary . . . . . . . . . . . . . . . . . . . . . . . . . . . . . . . . . . . . . . . . . . . . . . . . . .2-11
Review/Test Preparation . . . . . . . . . . . . . . . . . . . . . . . . . . . . . . . . . . . . . .2-12
Worksheet . . . . . . . . . . . . . . . . . . . . . . . . . . . . . . . . . . . . . . . . . . . . . . . . . . .2-14
Discussion . . . . . . . . . . . . . . . . . . . . . . . . . . . . . . . . . . . . . . . . . . . . . . . . . . .2-16
Activities . . . . . . . . . . . . . . . . . . . . . . . . . . . . . . . . . . . . . . . . . . . . . . . . . . . .2-17

**Chapter 3: BRAIN, BODY, AND BEHAVIOR**

Vocabulary . . . . . . . . . . . . . . . . . . . . . . . . . . . . . . . . . . . . . . . . . . . . . . . . . .3-19
Review/Test Preparation . . . . . . . . . . . . . . . . . . . . . . . . . . . . . . . . . . . . . .3-23
Worksheet . . . . . . . . . . . . . . . . . . . . . . . . . . . . . . . . . . . . . . . . . . . . . . . . . . .3-26
Discussion . . . . . . . . . . . . . . . . . . . . . . . . . . . . . . . . . . . . . . . . . . . . . . . . . . .3-27
Activities . . . . . . . . . . . . . . . . . . . . . . . . . . . . . . . . . . . . . . . . . . . . . . . . . . . .3-28

**Chapter 4: SENSATION AND PERCEPTION**

Vocabulary . . . . . . . . . . . . . . . . . . . . . . . . . . . . . . . . . . . . . . . . . . . . . . . . . .4-29
Review/Test Preparation . . . . . . . . . . . . . . . . . . . . . . . . . . . . . . . . . . . . . .4-32
Worksheet . . . . . . . . . . . . . . . . . . . . . . . . . . . . . . . . . . . . . . . . . . . . . . . . . . .4-35
Discussion . . . . . . . . . . . . . . . . . . . . . . . . . . . . . . . . . . . . . . . . . . . . . . . . . . .4-36
Activities . . . . . . . . . . . . . . . . . . . . . . . . . . . . . . . . . . . . . . . . . . . . . . . . . . . .4-37

**Chapter 5: MOTIVATION AND EMOTION**

Vocabulary . . . . . . . . . . . . . . . . . . . . . . . . . . . . . . . . . . . . . . . . . . . . . . . . . .5-39
Review/Test Preparation . . . . . . . . . . . . . . . . . . . . . . . . . . . . . . . . . . . . . .5-42
Worksheet . . . . . . . . . . . . . . . . . . . . . . . . . . . . . . . . . . . . . . . . . . . . . . . . . . .5-43
Discussion . . . . . . . . . . . . . . . . . . . . . . . . . . . . . . . . . . . . . . . . . . . . . . . . . . .5-45
Activities . . . . . . . . . . . . . . . . . . . . . . . . . . . . . . . . . . . . . . . . . . . . . . . . . . . .5-46

**Chapter 6: STATES OF CONSCIOUSNESS**

Vocabulary . . . . . . . . . . . . . . . . . . . . . . . . . . . . . . . . . . . . . . . . . . . . . . . . . .6-49
Review/Test Preparation . . . . . . . . . . . . . . . . . . . . . . . . . . . . . . . . . . . . . .6-52
Worksheet . . . . . . . . . . . . . . . . . . . . . . . . . . . . . . . . . . . . . . . . . . . . . . . . . . .6-56
Discussion . . . . . . . . . . . . . . . . . . . . . . . . . . . . . . . . . . . . . . . . . . . . . . . . . . .6-57
Activities . . . . . . . . . . . . . . . . . . . . . . . . . . . . . . . . . . . . . . . . . . . . . . . . . . . .6-58

## Chapter 7:  PRINCIPLES OF LEARNING

Vocabulary . . . . . . . . . . . . . . . . . . . . . . . . . . . . . . . . . . . . . . . . . . .7-61

Review/Test Preparation . . . . . . . . . . . . . . . . . . . . . . . . . . . . . . .7-64

Worksheet . . . . . . . . . . . . . . . . . . . . . . . . . . . . . . . . . . . . . . . . . . .7-67

Discussion . . . . . . . . . . . . . . . . . . . . . . . . . . . . . . . . . . . . . . . . . . .7-68

Activities . . . . . . . . . . . . . . . . . . . . . . . . . . . . . . . . . . . . . . . . . . . .7-69

## Chapter 8:  ACQUIRING, PROCESSING, AND RETAINING INFORMATION

Vocabulary . . . . . . . . . . . . . . . . . . . . . . . . . . . . . . . . . . . . . . . . . . .8-75

Review/Test Preparation . . . . . . . . . . . . . . . . . . . . . . . . . . . . . . .8-77

Worksheet . . . . . . . . . . . . . . . . . . . . . . . . . . . . . . . . . . . . . . . . . . .8-81

Discussion . . . . . . . . . . . . . . . . . . . . . . . . . . . . . . . . . . . . . . . . . . .8-83

Activities . . . . . . . . . . . . . . . . . . . . . . . . . . . . . . . . . . . . . . . . . . . .8-84

## Chapter 9:  INTELLIGENCE AND CREATIVITY

Vocabulary . . . . . . . . . . . . . . . . . . . . . . . . . . . . . . . . . . . . . . . . . . .9-85

Review/Test Preparation . . . . . . . . . . . . . . . . . . . . . . . . . . . . . . .9-87

Worksheet . . . . . . . . . . . . . . . . . . . . . . . . . . . . . . . . . . . . . . . . . . .9-90

Discussion . . . . . . . . . . . . . . . . . . . . . . . . . . . . . . . . . . . . . . . . . . .9-91

Activities . . . . . . . . . . . . . . . . . . . . . . . . . . . . . . . . . . . . . . . . . . . .9-92

## Chapter 10:  INFANCY AND CHILDHOOD

Vocabulary . . . . . . . . . . . . . . . . . . . . . . . . . . . . . . . . . . . . . . . . . .10-95

Review/Test Preparation . . . . . . . . . . . . . . . . . . . . . . . . . . . . . .10-97

Worksheet . . . . . . . . . . . . . . . . . . . . . . . . . . . . . . . . . . . . . . . . .10-100

Discussion . . . . . . . . . . . . . . . . . . . . . . . . . . . . . . . . . . . . . . . . .10-101

Activities . . . . . . . . . . . . . . . . . . . . . . . . . . . . . . . . . . . . . . . . . .10-103

## Chapter 11:  ADOLESCENCE

Vocabulary . . . . . . . . . . . . . . . . . . . . . . . . . . . . . . . . . . . . . . . . .11-105

Review/Test Preparation . . . . . . . . . . . . . . . . . . . . . . . . . . . . . .11-107

Worksheet . . . . . . . . . . . . . . . . . . . . . . . . . . . . . . . . . . . . . . . . .11-110

Discussion . . . . . . . . . . . . . . . . . . . . . . . . . . . . . . . . . . . . . . . . .11-111

Activities . . . . . . . . . . . . . . . . . . . . . . . . . . . . . . . . . . . . . . . . . .11-113

## Chapter 12:  ADULTHOOD AND AGING

Vocabulary . . . . . . . . . . . . . . . . . . . . . . . . . . . . . . . . . . . . . . . . .12-115

Review/Test Preparation . . . . . . . . . . . . . . . . . . . . . . . . . . . . . .12-116

Worksheet . . . . . . . . . . . . . . . . . . . . . . . . . . . . . . . . . . . . . . . . .12-118

Discussion . . . . . . . . . . . . . . . . . . . . . . . . . . . . . . . . . . . . . . . . .12-120

Activities . . . . . . . . . . . . . . . . . . . . . . . . . . . . . . . . . . . . . . . . . .12-122

## Chapter 13:  GENDER DIFFERENCES

Vocabulary . . . . . . . . . . . . . . . . . . . . . . . . . . . . . . . . . . . . . . . . .13-125

Review/Test Preparation . . . . . . . . . . . . . . . . . . . . . . . . . . . . . .13-127

Worksheet . . . . . . . . . . . . . . . . . . . . . . . . . . . . . . . . . . . . . . . . .13-130

Discussion . . . . . . . . . . . . . . . . . . . . . . . . . . . . . . . . . . . . . . . . .13-131

Activities . . . . . . . . . . . . . . . . . . . . . . . . . . . . . . . . . . . . . . . . . .13-132

## Chapter 14: THEORIES OF PERSONALITY

Vocabulary . . . . . . . . . . . . . . . . . . . . . . . . . . . . . .14-135
Review/Test Preparation . . . . . . . . . . . . . . . . . . . .14-137
Worksheet . . . . . . . . . . . . . . . . . . . . . . . . . . . . . .14-140
Discussion . . . . . . . . . . . . . . . . . . . . . . . . . . . . . .14-141
Activities . . . . . . . . . . . . . . . . . . . . . . . . . . . . . . .14-142

## Chapter 15: MEASURING PERSONALITY AND PERSONAL ABILITIES

Vocabulary . . . . . . . . . . . . . . . . . . . . . . . . . . . . . .15-145
Review/Test Preparation . . . . . . . . . . . . . . . . . . . .15-148
Worksheet . . . . . . . . . . . . . . . . . . . . . . . . . . . . . .15-150
Discussion . . . . . . . . . . . . . . . . . . . . . . . . . . . . . .15-152
Activities . . . . . . . . . . . . . . . . . . . . . . . . . . . . . . .15-153

## Chapter 16: FRUSTRATION, CONFLICT, STRESS, AND DRUGS

Vocabulary . . . . . . . . . . . . . . . . . . . . . . . . . . . . . .16-155
Review/Test Preparation . . . . . . . . . . . . . . . . . . . .16-158
Worksheet . . . . . . . . . . . . . . . . . . . . . . . . . . . . . .16-160
Discussion . . . . . . . . . . . . . . . . . . . . . . . . . . . . . .16-163
Activities . . . . . . . . . . . . . . . . . . . . . . . . . . . . . . .16-164

## Chapter 17: TOWARD A HEALTHY PERSONALITY

Vocabulary . . . . . . . . . . . . . . . . . . . . . . . . . . . . . .17-167
Review/Test Preparation . . . . . . . . . . . . . . . . . . . .17-170
Worksheet . . . . . . . . . . . . . . . . . . . . . . . . . . . . . .17-172
Discussion . . . . . . . . . . . . . . . . . . . . . . . . . . . . . .17-174
Activities . . . . . . . . . . . . . . . . . . . . . . . . . . . . . . .17-176

## Chapter 18: TREATMENT AND THERAPY

Vocabulary . . . . . . . . . . . . . . . . . . . . . . . . . . . . . .18-177
Review/Test Preparation . . . . . . . . . . . . . . . . . . . .18-179
Worksheet . . . . . . . . . . . . . . . . . . . . . . . . . . . . . .18-181
Discussion . . . . . . . . . . . . . . . . . . . . . . . . . . . . . .18-182
Activities . . . . . . . . . . . . . . . . . . . . . . . . . . . . . . .18-183

## Chapter 19: SOCIOCULTURAL INFLUENCES AND RELATIONSHIPS

Vocabulary . . . . . . . . . . . . . . . . . . . . . . . . . . . . . .19-185
Review/Test Preparation . . . . . . . . . . . . . . . . . . . .19-187
Worksheet . . . . . . . . . . . . . . . . . . . . . . . . . . . . . .19-189
Discussion . . . . . . . . . . . . . . . . . . . . . . . . . . . . . .19-191
Activities . . . . . . . . . . . . . . . . . . . . . . . . . . . . . . .19-192

## Chapter 20: SOCIOCULTURAL INFLUENCES: ATTITUDES AND BELIEFS

Vocabulary . . . . . . . . . . . . . . . . . . . . . . . . . . . . . .20-193
Review/Test Preparation . . . . . . . . . . . . . . . . . . . .20-195
Worksheet . . . . . . . . . . . . . . . . . . . . . . . . . . . . . .20-196
Discussion . . . . . . . . . . . . . . . . . . . . . . . . . . . . . .20-198
Activities . . . . . . . . . . . . . . . . . . . . . . . . . . . . . . .20-199

Name _____ Date _____ Period _____

# Chapter 1   The Field of Psychology

---

## VOCABULARY

---

**DIRECTIONS:** Define the following terms using complete sentences:

1. psychology _____

   _____

2. research psychologists _____

   _____

3. applied psychologists _____

   _____

4. theory _____

   _____

5. introspection _____

   _____

6. eclecticism _____

   _____

7. biopsychological approach _____

   _____

8. behavioral approach _____

   _____

9. humanistic approach _____

   _____

10. psychoanalysis _____

    _____

11. cognitive approach _____

    _____

12. sociocultural approach _____

    _____

---

# REVIEW/TEST PREPARATION

**MULTIPLE CHOICE:** Write the letter of the correct answer in the space provided.

_____ 1. Psychology is the scientific study of
    a. man and animal behavior.
    b. mental processes and behavior.
    c. laboratory animals.
    d. how stars affect behavior.

_____ 2. Behavior includes
    a. only observable acts by organisms.
    b. one's intention as expressed in body language.
    c. almost any activity.
    d. the interaction between and among humans.

_____ 3. Two basic types of psychologists are
    a. behavioral and cognitive psychologists.
    b. research and applied psychologists.
    c. laboratory and field psychologists.
    d. psychoanalysts and humanists.

_____ 4. The "father of psychology" is
    a. Sigmund Freud.
    b. Wilhelm Wundt.
    c. B. F. Skinner.
    d. Carl Rogers.

_____ 5. Freud's theory of personality is based on
    a. conscious interaction among people.
    b. conflicts which people have with others.
    c. the effects of unconscious conflicts within the individual.
    d. conscious memories which cause mental illnesses.

_____ 6. One of the founders of American psychology was
    a. B. F. Skinner.
    b. William James.
    c. Sigmund Freud.
    d. Charles Watson.

_____ 7. The approach to the study based on the effects of unconscious conflicts within the individual is know as the
    a. psychoanalytic approach.
    b. cognitive approach.
    c. behavioral approach.
    d. sociocultural approach.

_____  8.  The approach which examines behavior in terms of the physical changes that take place is known as the
   a.  behavioral approach.
   b.  cognitive approach.
   c.  biopsychological approach.
   d.  humanistic approach.

_____  9.  The first laboratory for studying humans was established in
   a.  1879.
   b.  1854.
   c.  1897.
   d.  1876.

_____  10.  The process for studying humans used by Wundt is called
   a.  involution.
   b.  mesmerism.
   c.  hypnotism.
   d.  introspection.

_____  11.  Psychologists who borrow from other theories to make their own combination are using
   a.  plagiarism.
   b.  behaviorism.
   c.  humanism.
   d.  eclecticism.

_____  12.  The psychological theory which views behavior as strongly influenced by psychological functions is
   a.  behavioral.
   b.  biopsychological.
   c.  physiological.
   d.  psychoanalytical.

_____  13.  Psychologists who believe that we are the result of stimulus-response situations are called
   a.  S-R psychologists.
   b.  humanists.
   c.  behaviorists.
   d.  S-R analysts.

_____  14.  The most famous behaviorist today is
   a.  Carl Rogers.
   b.  B. F. Skinner.
   c.  Sigmund Freud.
   d.  Wilhelm Wundt.

_____ 15. An approach to human behavior which came into being in reaction to behaviorism
is the
a. humanistic approach.
b. cognitive approach.
c. psychoanalytic approach.
d. physiological approach.

_____ 16. The person who developed the psychoanalytic approach to studying behavior is
a. B. F. Skinner.
b. Sigmund Freud.
c. Wilhelm Wundt.
d. Carl Rogers.

_____ 17. The approach to the study of behavior which emphasizes one's thinking or use of
mental processes is the
a. psychoanalytic approach.
b. humanistic approach.
c. behavioral approach.
d. cognitive approach.

_____ 18. The psychologist who suggested that humans be studied as complete wholes was
a. John B. Watson.
b. William James.
c. B. F. Skinner.
d. Carl Rogers.

_____ 19. The psychologist who suggested that we are influenced by childhood experiences
and unconscious forces was
a. Wilhelm Wundt.
b. Carl Rogers.
c. Sigmund Freud.
d. B. F. Skinner.

_____ 20. The psychologist who emphasized the positive side of human nature was
a. William James.
b. B. F. Skinner.
c. Wilhelm Wundt.
d. Carl Rogers.

# WORKSHEET

**DIRECTIONS:** Complete the crossword puzzle.

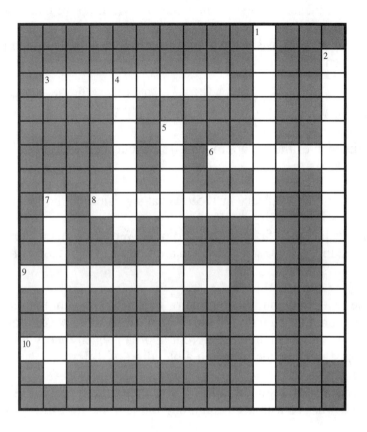

**ACROSS**
5. Making one's own system by borrowing from two or more other systems
3. Person who believes that people are basically good and capable of helping themselves
6. System of viewing the individual as the product of an unconscious; _____ analysis
8. Type of psychology which studies the origin, cause, or results of certain behaviors
9. Type of psychology which emphasizes using mental processes to handle problems or develop certain personality characteristics
10. Those who believe we are the product of associations; _____ists

**DOWN**
1. Type of psychology which views behavior as strongly influenced by physiological functions
2. Looking into oneself and describing what is there
4. Type of psychology which makes direct use of the findings of research psychologists; deals directly with clients
7. General frameworks for scientific studies

# DISCUSSION

1. A good definition for psychology which covers the many things psychologists do is that it is the scientific study of mental processes and behavior. What do we mean by *scientific* study?

2. Two basic types of psychologists are research psychologists and applied psychologists. Differentiate between these types.

3. Write a short description on the contributions each of the following men have made to the field of psychology: Wilhelm Wundt, Sigmund Freud, William James, and John B. Watson.

4. Name and explain each of the six approaches to psychology which are listed in this first chapter.

5. Charles Darwin published his theory in 1859. What significance did this have for psychology?

6. Wilhelm Wundt is called the "father of psychology." What was his reasoning and the method of research he used in this first scientific research into the behavior of man? Why was his method unsuccessful?

7. The author of the text points out that the major theories of psychology appear to contradict each other, but the fact that they do not agree is all right since we do not have the final answer on human nature. Explain the different approach each theory takes and how an eclectic psychologist might effectively use a blending of different aspects of each.

8. The field of psychology offers many different occupational possibilities; several are listed in the text. Discuss what contributions one may make in each of these areas.

Name _____ Date _____ Period _____

## ACTIVITIES

### TAKE A CRUISE INTO THE HISTORY OF PSYCHOLOGY

Psychology as a separate science is just over one hundred years old. Yet, as long as humans have existed, they have been curious about their own behavior. Get aboard for a cruise through the history of humanity's efforts to explain itself and you will arrive at the present day status of one of the most interesting of all sciences, PSYCHOLOGY.

1.  We begin at the beginning. What does the word *psychology* mean?

    Scientific study of the emotions                      Sail to Pier 10
    Scientific study of mental processes and behavior     Sail to Pier 6

2.  There are two basic types of psychologists. They are

    Research and applied psychologists                    Sail to Pier 7
    Behavioral and eclectic psychologists                 Sail to Pier 12

3.  Sorry. Engineering psychologists work to design systems that help people become more efficient. Cruise on back to Pier 8 and try another port of call.

4.  Wrong port! Restock your provisions and go back to Pier 13.

5.  In the latter half of the 1800s, psychology came into being as a separate science. The person responsible for this was

    Charles Darwin                                        Sail to Pier 14
    Wilhelm Wundt                                         Sail to Pier 20

6.  Good, you are in the right port! Psychology is the scientific study of mental processes and behavior. Cruise on to #8.

7.  Welcome ashore - this is the right pier. The two types of psychologists are research and applied psychologists. Research psychologists study the origin, cause, or results of certain behaviors. Applied psychologists make direct use of (apply) psychological studies. Get aboard quickly, for now we sail to Pier 5.

8.  Psychologists who work in industry or university settings are called

    Experimental psychologists                            Sail to Pier 11
    Engineering psychologists                             Sail to Pier 3

9.  Too bad! Wrong port again. Check your fresh water supply and return to Pier 13.

10. Sorry. Too bad you missed the boat this time. However, don't give up the ship. Go back to Pier 1 and try again.

11. Right ho, mate. Experimental psychologists perform research to understand better how the human operates physically or psychologically. Your next port of call is Pier 13.

12. Too bad, but you are miles away from your designated pier. Make sure supplies are plentiful and sail back to Pier 2.

13. An early psychologist who created learning theories that are widely applied, even today, is

    | | |
    |---|---|
    | Charles Darwin | Sail to Pier 4 |
    | Carl Rogers | Sail to Pier 9 |
    | John B. Watson | Sail to Pier 16 |

14. No, sorry! Charles Darwin's efforts did start scientists studying animal behavior in order to try to better understand human behavior, but this was before the date of the birth of psychology. Darwin's theory has been generating arguments and disputes since it was published in 1859. Back to Pier 5 for another try.

15. Since its infantile beginnings in 1879, psychology has grown into a fully matured science. At the present time there are six approaches to the nature of the human. However, some scientists do not rigidly adhere to one or the other of these, but choose parts from the other theories to make their own system. This is called

    | | |
    |---|---|
    | Behaviorism | Sail to Pier 9 |
    | Eclecticism | Sail to Pier 21 |
    | Humanistic | Sail to Pier 24 |

16. Now you've got it. John B. Watson, who studied learning during the 1920s, is the one who created learning theories which are still widely applied. For another fascinating tour, try docking at Pier 2.

17. Good! You've docked at the right pier. Sigmund Freud developed the psychoanalytic theory. He placed much emphasis on the effects of the unconscious. You will learn more about this as you sail on through the text. Now go to Pier 27.

18. The best known of all the theories, the one which considers the inner self to be a cesspool of forbidden desires, is

    | | |
    |---|---|
    | Psychoanalysis | Sail to Pier 17 |
    | Biopsychological | Sail to Pier 22 |
    | Cognitive | Sail to Pier 26 |

19. Behaviorism focuses strictly on the behavior of animals and humans. Sorry, wrong pier. Back to dock at Pier 15.

20. Welcome to this lovely island! Indeed it was Wilhelm Wundt who, in 1879, started the first laboratory in Leipzig, Germany, for studying humans. The method he used was introspection, so called because one looks into oneself and tells what is there. This method is still used, though in a different way from Wundt's early efforts. Cruise back to your text for more information on this one. Time to board again, for now we are off to Pier 15 as we set sail for more present day psychology history.

21. Good choice! While most psychologists tend to adhere to one of the six theories, they do borrow aspects from the others, making their own combination, called eclecticism. Now we sail on to Pier 18.

22. Ooops! Wrong pier. The biopsychological approach deals with the study of mental processes and behavior. They explain behavior in terms of the physical changes that take place. Now, sail back to Pier 18 for a change in course.

23. Sorrreee! A clinical/counseling psychologist works with people who have marital, personal, or mental problems. Return to the port of origin for this question, 27.

24. Wrong pier again. Humanism arose as a reaction to the behavioristic theory, which you will explore in more detail in the text. Happy sailing! Now return to Pier 15 for further instruction.

25. Again, wrong one. A developmental/child psychologist studies the development of the child and also may work in a clinic or private practice to help disturbed children and/or their parents. Sail on back to Pier 27 for a recharting of your craft.

26. Missed the right port of call. The cognitive approach emphasizes the use of mental processes. We are thinking creatures and therefore able to reason and think through problems and situations. More about this later in your journey. Now, check supplies again and set sail for a return to Pier 18.

27. Today everyone is a psychologist—called arm-chair psychologist (for obvious reasons). If you want to go into a psychological field wherein you will be involved with things of an educational nature, you would choose

| | |
|---|---|
| Clinical/Counseling psychology | Sail to Pier 23 |
| Developmental/Child psychology | Sail to Pier 25 |
| School/Educational psychology | Sail to Pier 29 |

28. That's right! Introspection is the process of looking into yourself and describing what is there. The cruise is over.

29. You've made the nautical ranks. School/educational psychologists may work in the school setting helping design and improve school curricula, or working directly with students. We hope you have had a wonderful cruise and that you will join us again. Now, before you debark, conclude your trip at Pier 30.

30. Congratulations! Your trip is over. Here are the ports which would give the shortest journey: 1, 6, 8, 11, 13, 16, 2, 7, 5, 20, 15, 21, 18, 17, 27, 29 and 30. Did you have a short trip? Hope you had a fabulous time. Before you go, how about one more side trip? Can you define the term *introspection*? See Pier 28 for the answer.

Name _____ Date _____ Period _____

# Chapter 2    *Methods of Psychology*

• • • • • • • • • • • • • • • • • • • • • • • • • • • • • • • • • • • • •

## VOCABULARY

**MATCHING:** Choose the appropriate vocabulary word and place the letter in the space provided.

a. placebo
b. hypothesis
c. subjects
d. variables
e. dependent variable
f. independent variable
g. field study
h. experimental group
i. control group

j. survey
k. sample
l. naturalistic observation
m. interview
n. case study method
o. psychological tests
p. cross-sectional method
q. longitudinal method
r. double-blind study

_____ 1. Developing information about one's background, usually for psychological treatment.

_____ 2. The group that does not have the critical part of the experiment done to them.

_____ 3. That which the researcher changes or varies in a study.

_____ 4. Neither participants nor researchers know to which group any subject belongs.

_____ 5. A group that represents a larger group.

_____ 6. Statement of the results the experimenter expected to get.

_____ 7. Things that can change or vary in an experiment.

_____ 8. The group upon which the critical part of the experiment is performed.

_____ 9. Studying people face to face and asking questions.

_____ 10. A method of research using different age groups at the same time in order to understand changes during the life span.

_____ 11. Studying the same group of people over an extended period of time.

_____ 12. Method of research using questions of feelings, opinions, or behavior patterns.

_____ 13. Research outside the laboratory, "in the field."

_____ 14. The factor in a study that changes or varies as a result of changes in the other variable.

_____ 15. A "medicine" which has no active ingredients and works by the power of suggestion.

_____ 16. People or animals on which the research is done.

_____ 17. Observation and measurement of subject using objective measures.

_____ 18. Studying subjects without their being aware that they are being watched.

# REVIEW/TEST PREPARATION

**A.  TRUE/FALSE:**  Write **T** if the statement is true or **F** if the statement is false.

_____  1.  It is difficult to draw meaningful conclusions without very careful experimentation.

_____  2.  Placebos are effective because the person believes they will help.

_____  3.  There is a direct relationship between phases of the moon and our behavior.

_____  4.  One way to overcome bias in an interview is to use objective psychological tests such as the IQ.

_____  5.  Psychological tests are objective methods of gathering information on people.

**B.  MULTIPLE CHOICE:**  Write the letter of the correct answer in the space provided.

_____  1.  In an experiment, the hypothesis is a statement
    a.  of the findings.
    b.  based on fact.
    c.  proven true.
    d.  of the expected results.

_____  2.  Every experiment has variables, or things that can change or vary. The variable that will change depending on another factor is the
    a.  independent variable.
    b.  dependent variable.
    c.  intervening variable.
    d.  control variable.

_____  3.  A variable that is examined in order to determine its effects on behavior is the
    a.  independent variable.
    b.  dependent variable.
    c.  intervening variable.
    d.  control variable.

_____  4.  Experiments conducted in laboratories or in the field usually involve two groups, called
    a.  dependent and independent groups.
    b.  dependent and independent subjects.
    c.  control and experimental groups.
    d.  control and neutral subjects.

_____  5.  Since everyone cannot be interviewed in a survey, a certain number of people are chosen to represent the general population. This is called a
    a.  control group.
    b.  experimental group.
    c.  sample.
    d.  subject.

Name _____ Date _____ Period _____

---

C. **COMPLETION:** Write the missing word(s) in the blank.

1. A _____ involves gathering information by asking questions either by mail, in person, or over the telephone.

2. Researchers who secretly observe the object of the study in a natural setting use the _____ method of collecting data.

3. Another method for collecting data for studying people and their past histories is the _____ .

4. The method which involves developing information about a person's background for purposes of psychological treatment is the _____ method.

5. Researchers who study patterns of behavior over a period of time to determine any changes may use one of two methods, the _____ method, or the _____ method.

6. In the _____ method, the same subjects are studied over a long period of time, which involves considerable expense.

7. The _____ method uses people from different age groups and is thus less expensive and time-consuming.

8. Guidelines established by the American Psychological Association regarding experiments are called _____ .

9. One area of difference between males and females is called _____ .

10. Experiments conducted away from a laboratory setting are called _____ _____ .

# WORKSHEET

**DIRECTIONS:** Unscramble the words on the left to find the solution to the questions on the right.

N A T I S

$\overline{9}$ $\overline{2}$ $\overline{8}$ $\overline{1}$ $\overline{3}$

A L U R M

$\overline{\phantom{0}}$ $\overline{4}$ $\overline{5}$ $\overline{6}$ $\overline{7}$

C A T I N

$\overline{\phantom{0}}$ $\overline{\phantom{0}}$ $\overline{10}$ $\overline{11}$ $\overline{12}$

1. Which method of research is used when the researchers secretly observe the subject in daily activity in its natural surroundings?

$\overline{1}$ $\overline{2}$ $\overline{3}$ $\overline{4}$ $\overline{5}$ $\overline{6}$ $\overline{7}$ $\overline{8}$ $\overline{9}$ $\overline{10}$ $\overline{11}$ $\overline{12}$

---

G U N S T

$\overline{1}$ $\overline{9}$ $\overline{2}$ $\overline{\phantom{0}}$ $\overline{\phantom{0}}$

L E A V H E N Y

$\overline{10}$ $\overline{5}$ $\overline{\phantom{0}}$ $\overline{4}$ $\overline{8}$ $\overline{\phantom{0}}$ $\overline{\phantom{0}}$ $\overline{6}$

M O R D

$\overline{12}$ $\overline{11}$ $\overline{3}$ $\overline{7}$

2. When one collects data by asking questions by mail, in person, or over the phone, which method is used?

$\overline{1}$ $\overline{2}$ $\overline{3}$ $\overline{4}$ $\overline{5}$ $\overline{6}$    $\overline{7}$ $\overline{8}$ $\overline{9}$ $\overline{10}$ $\overline{11}$ $\overline{12}$

---

V E N N I T

$\overline{1}$ $\overline{2}$ $\overline{6}$ $\overline{4}$ $\overline{\phantom{0}}$ $\overline{3}$

A R W E Y

$\overline{9}$ $\overline{8}$ $\overline{\phantom{0}}$ $\overline{\phantom{0}}$ $\overline{\phantom{0}}$

T R I S T H

$\overline{\phantom{0}}$ $\overline{\phantom{0}}$ $\overline{7}$ $\overline{5}$ $\overline{\phantom{0}}$ $\overline{\phantom{0}}$

3. What is the common method for studying people and their past histories?

$\overline{1}$ $\overline{2}$ $\overline{3}$ $\overline{4}$ $\overline{5}$ $\overline{6}$ $\overline{7}$ $\overline{8}$ $\overline{9}$

D E S A T E

$\overline{\phantom{x}}$ $\overline{\phantom{x}}$ $\overline{\phantom{x}}$ $\overline{\phantom{x}}$ $\overline{\phantom{x}}$ $\overline{\phantom{x}}$
3  4  8  2  6

M U S C O T

$\overline{\phantom{x}}$ $\overline{\phantom{x}}$ $\overline{\phantom{x}}$ $\overline{\phantom{x}}$ $\overline{\phantom{x}}$ $\overline{\phantom{x}}$
1  7  5

D Y T I

$\overline{\phantom{x}}$ $\overline{\phantom{x}}$ $\overline{\phantom{x}}$ $\overline{\phantom{x}}$
        9

4. Developing information about a person's background for purposes of psychological treatment would utilize which method?

$\overline{\phantom{x}}$ $\overline{\phantom{x}}$ $\overline{\phantom{x}}$ $\overline{\phantom{x}}$    $\overline{\phantom{x}}$ $\overline{\phantom{x}}$ $\overline{\phantom{x}}$ $\overline{\phantom{x}}$ $\overline{\phantom{x}}$
1  2  3  4    5  6  7  8  9

T U I T D A T E

$\overline{\phantom{x}}$ $\overline{\phantom{x}}$ $\overline{\phantom{x}}$ $\overline{\phantom{x}}$ $\overline{\phantom{x}}$ $\overline{\phantom{x}}$ $\overline{\phantom{x}}$ $\overline{\phantom{x}}$
        5  6  7  8

L E A N I D

$\overline{\phantom{x}}$ $\overline{\phantom{x}}$ $\overline{\phantom{x}}$ $\overline{\phantom{x}}$ $\overline{\phantom{x}}$ $\overline{\phantom{x}}$
    10  9  11  12

B L E G O N

$\overline{\phantom{x}}$ $\overline{\phantom{x}}$ $\overline{\phantom{x}}$ $\overline{\phantom{x}}$ $\overline{\phantom{x}}$ $\overline{\phantom{x}}$
    1  2  3  4

5. This study would involve examining the same group of people over and over during a long period of time. What is it?

$\overline{\phantom{x}}$ $\overline{\phantom{x}}$ $\overline{\phantom{x}}$ $\overline{\phantom{x}}$ $\overline{\phantom{x}}$ $\overline{\phantom{x}}$ $\overline{\phantom{x}}$ $\overline{\phantom{x}}$ $\overline{\phantom{x}}$ $\overline{\phantom{x}}$ $\overline{\phantom{x}}$ $\overline{\phantom{x}}$
1  2  3  4  5  6  7  8  9  10  11  12

O C A T I N

$\overline{\phantom{x}}$ $\overline{\phantom{x}}$ $\overline{\phantom{x}}$ $\overline{\phantom{x}}$ $\overline{\phantom{x}}$ $\overline{\phantom{x}}$
  1    10  3  12

A S O N S E A L

$\overline{\phantom{x}}$ $\overline{\phantom{x}}$ $\overline{\phantom{x}}$ $\overline{\phantom{x}}$ $\overline{\phantom{x}}$ $\overline{\phantom{x}}$ $\overline{\phantom{x}}$
5  7    6  11    13  14

S T E R C

$\overline{\phantom{x}}$ $\overline{\phantom{x}}$ $\overline{\phantom{x}}$ $\overline{\phantom{x}}$ $\overline{\phantom{x}}$
8  2    4  9

6. This method studies the effects of time by using people from different age groups at one time. What is it?

$\overline{\phantom{x}}$ $\overline{\phantom{x}}$ $\overline{\phantom{x}}$ $\overline{\phantom{x}}$ $\overline{\phantom{x}}$ $\overline{\phantom{x}}$ $\overline{\phantom{x}}$ $\overline{\phantom{x}}$ $\overline{\phantom{x}}$ $\overline{\phantom{x}}$ $\overline{\phantom{x}}$ $\overline{\phantom{x}}$ $\overline{\phantom{x}}$ $\overline{\phantom{x}}$
1  2  3  4  5  6  7  8  9  10  11  12  13  14

# DISCUSSION

1. Many people not only read their horoscopes daily, but place great faith in their accuracy. People in ancient times believed we were ruled by heavenly bodies. Discuss the research done on the effects of the phases of the moon on behavior. What did the research show? Do you agree or disagree with these findings?

2. What are some problems which could interfere with obtaining completely accurate results in naturalistic observation involving humans?

3. Who should decide what is harmful to subjects and what is not harmful to subjects in an experiment?

4. Would you participate in an experiment? Why or why not?

5. How do research or experimental psychologists differ from other types of psychologists?

6. Name and describe some of the different ways in which psychologists collect data.

7. Why is a control group necessary in experiments? What is the criteria for selecting the control group?

8. Explain the interaction of the dependent and the independent variables.

9. Differentiate between longitudinal and cross-sectional studies. Why may one choose to use the cross-sectional method over the longitudinal method of study?

10. What is a hypothesis? Is it always proven to be true or correct? Why or why not?

## ACTIVITIES

1. Interview one of your good friends about his or her use of leisure time. Make up about ten questions relating to school activities, sports, television viewing, movies, hobbies, and other recreation. Keep notes as you interview the person.

2. *National Geographic* often has features on naturalistic observation. Search through some back issues of this magazine to find one of these and read the article. Find out what the purpose of the observation was, how the experimenter went about collecting data, and the results of the study.

3. To get more information on laboratory experiments, check through some back issues of *Psychology Today.* After you have found one, read the experiment and answer the following: What was the hypothesis? The control group, if applicable? The experimental group? The independent variable? Dependent variable? Any intervening variables?

4. The American Psychological Association has established guidelines called Ethical Principles that relate to experiments involving humans. Make up a list of guidelines you would like to see used in experiments which involve animals.

5. For your own naturalistic observation experiment, sit in the lobby of a hotel, in a bus terminal, a train station, or an airport, and write down your observations of how people behave. How do the people react when greeting each other? How do they react to strangers? How do they react to time delays, either in departure or if waiting for someone to arrive? When you have written your observations, ask your teacher to check it for subjective statements which have no supporting data. Through this exercise you will be able to learn to be more objective in your observations.

Name _____ Date _____ Period _____

# Chapter 3    Brain, Body, and Behavior

## VOCABULARY

**DIRECTIONS:** Fill in the blanks with the correct word or phrase from the following vocabulary list. Not all of the words will be used.

| | | |
|---|---|---|
| cerebral cortex | amygdala | parasympathetic nervous system |
| fissure | hippocampus | reflex |
| hemisphere | hypothalamus | peripheral nervous system |
| corpus callosum | cerebellum | somatic nervous system |
| lobes | reticular activating system | autonomic nervous system |
| frontal lobe | (RAS) | hormones |
| motor strip | neuron | glands |
| sensory strip | dendrites | endocrine system |
| occipital lobe | axon | pituitary gland |
| temporal lobe | synapse | growth hormone |
| prefrontal area | vesicles | thyroid gland |
| frontal association area | neurotransmitters | metabolism |
| dominance | acetylcholine | adrenal glands |
| lower brain | dopamine | adrenaline |
| thalamus | endorphins | gonads |
| limbic system | central nervous system | androgen |
| sympathetic nervous | spinal cord | estrogen |
| system | | |

1. Term that indicates that for each person, one hemisphere is preferred and controls the majority of actions performed

   _____

2. The part of the neuron that carries messages away from the nerve cell to dendrites on another nerve cell

   _____

3. Portion of the brain that regulates basic needs (hunger, thirst) and emotions such as pleasure, fear, rage, sexuality

   _____

4. Chemical regulators that control the activity level of the glands

   _____

5. The gland that controls and regulates the speed of bodily processes, called metabolism

   _____

6. The sex glands that make sperm or eggs for reproduction

   _____

7. The outermost layer of the brain, controls very high-level thought

   _____

8. One half of the two halves of the brain; the right controls the left half of the body while the left controls the right side

   _____

9. The junction point of two or more neurons; connection is made by neurotransmitters

   _____

10. The speed with which the body operates

    _____

11. An automatic behavior of the body involving movement through the spinal cord without using the higher brain

    _____

12. The male sex hormone

    _____

13. The rectangular band running down the side of the brain which registers and provides all sensation

    _____

14. Massive bundle of nerve fibers that connects the two hemispheres

    _____

15. Chemical in the endings of nerve junctions that sends information across the synapse

    _____

16. Portion of the animal brain which coordinates and organizes bodily movements for balance and proper movement

    _____

17. Bodily units that contain the hormones

_____

18. Glands that cause excitement in order to prepare the body for an emergency or some important activity

_____

19. The female sex hormone

_____

20. The term for all the glands and their chemical messages taken together

_____

21. The alertness control center of the brain that regulates activity level of the body

_____

22. Functions as an automatic "brain" in its own right and is a relay station for impulses to and from the higher brain

_____

23. A neurotransmitter that is involved in motor functions or movement

_____

24. Part of the brain which contains the thalamus, cerebellum, hypothalamus, and the reticular activating system

_____

25. The chemical that prepares the body for emergency activity by increasing blood pressure, breathing rate, and energy level

_____

26. Master gland of the body which is attached to and controlled by the hypothalamus and controls growth and the growth hormone

_____

27. Nerve cell that transmits electrical and chemical information throughout the body

_____

28. Portion of the lower brain that functions primarily as a central relay station for incoming/outgoing messages from the body to the brain and from the brain to the body

_____

29. Forward portion of the brain which is very heavily packed with nerve cells because its task is to interpret what is going on and tells us how to react

_____

30. Hormone controlled by the pituitary that regulates the growth process

_____

31. Neurotransmitters that relieve pain and increase our sense of well-being

_____

32. The rectangular strip running down the side of the brain which controls all motor movements

_____

33. Part of the nerve cell that receives information from the axons of other nerve cells

_____

34. Contains structures involved in basic emotions and, to some extent, memory

_____

35. Lies outside the central nervous system and transmits messages between the central nervous system and all parts of the body

_____

Name _____ Date _____ Period _____

---

# REVIEW/TEST PREPARATION

---

**MULTIPLE CHOICE:** Write the letter of the correct answer in the space provided.

_____ 1. The brain is divided into halves. Each half is called a
     a. corpus callosum.
     b. hemisphere.
     c. thalamus.
     d. hypothalamus.

_____ 2. Along the top of the left hemisphere of the brain are located two rectangular areas, side by side, called
     a. visual and motor strips.
     b. neurons and motor strip.
     c. sensory and motor strips.
     d. frontal and sensory strips.

_____ 3. The speech area, for most people, is located in the
     a. left hemisphere.
     b. frontal lobe.
     c. right hemisphere.
     d. temporal lobe.

_____ 4. The visual area is located in the
     a. temporal part of the brain.
     b. back part of the brain.
     c. frontal part of the brain.
     d. top half of the brain.

_____ 5. Most people are
     a. right-hemisphere dominant, left handed.
     b. right-hemisphere dominant, right handed.
     c. left-hemisphere dominant, right handed.
     d. left-hemisphere dominant, left handed.

_____ 6. Intelligence for right- versus left-handed people is
     a. higher in right-handed people.
     b. higher in left-handed people.
     c. about the same for both groups.
     d. not known at present.

_____ 7. The part of the lower brain known as the relay station, receiving and sending messages to and from various parts of the brain, is the
     a. hypothalamus.
     b. reticular activating system.
     c. cerebellum.
     d. thalamus.

---

_____  8.  The part of the lower brain which coordinates muscle movements such as in walking and swimming is the
a.  hypothalamus.
b.  reticular activating system.
c.  cerebellum.
d.  thalamus.

_____  9.  The part of the lower brain which helps control rage, pleasure, hunger, thirst, and sexual desire is the
a.  hypothalamus.
b.  reticular activating system.
c.  cerebellum.
d.  thalamus.

_____  10.  The part of the lower brain which is the alertness control center of the brain and that regulates the activity level of the body is the
a.  hypothalamus.
b.  reticular activating system.
c.  cerebellum.
d.  thalamus.

_____  11.  Nerve cells are called
a.  axons.
b.  neurons.
c.  dendrites.
d.  reflexes.

_____  12.  The neural pathway is
a.  synapse, end of axon, dendrite.
b.  synapse, dendrite, end of axon.
c.  end of axon, synapse, dendrite.
d.  dendrite, synapse, end of axon.

_____  13.  The endocrine system is made up of
a.  muscles and glands.
b.  spinal cord and glands.
c.  muscles and metabolism.
d.  glands and chemical messages.

_____  14.  The master gland which secretes a growth hormone is the
a.  adrenal gland.
b.  thyroid gland.
c.  gonads.
d.  pituitary gland.

_____  15.  The gland which controls metabolism is the
a.  adrenal gland.
b.  thyroid gland.
c.  gonads.
d.  pituitary gland.

_____ 16. The gland which secretes adrenaline into the bloodstream in emergency situations is the
  a. adrenal gland.
  b. thyroid gland.
  c. gonads.
  d. pituitary gland.

_____ 17. The sex glands, which make the sperm and egg for reproduction, are the
  a. adrenal glands.
  b. thyroid glands.
  c. gonads.
  d. pituitary gland.

_____ 18. The male and female hormones are
  a. androgen and estrogen.
  b. androgen and adrenaline.
  c. adrenaline and estrogen.
  d. acetylcholine and estrogen.

_____ 19. The nerve fibers which connect the two hemispheres of the brain are called the
  a. corpus callosum.
  b. cerebellum.
  c. cortex.
  d. center brain.

_____ 20. The speed with which the body operates or the speed with which it uses up energy is called the
  a. endocrine system.
  b. dominance.
  c. metabolism.
  d. reflex.

_____ 21. The central nervous system consists of
  a. neurons of spinal cord and the brain.
  b. a spinal reflex and the brain stem.
  c. reflex zone and the pain center.
  d. peripheral nervous system and the brain.

_____ 22. The two main divisions of the peripheral nervous system are
  a. the nodal system and the reflex zone.
  b. the spinal cord and the cerebral cortex.
  c. the endocrine system and the cerebellum.
  d. the somatic nervous system and the autonomic nervous system.

Name _____ Date _____ Period _____

# WORKSHEET

**DIRECTIONS:** Label the parts of the brain and endocrine system below.

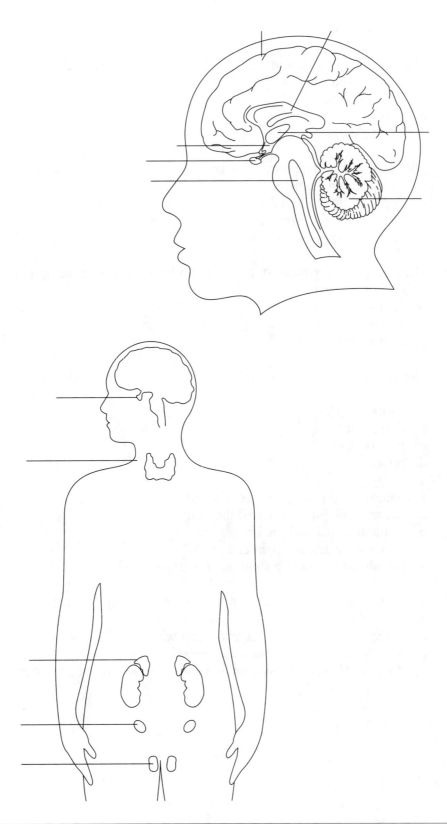

## DISCUSSION

1.  The brain is divided into two hemispheres, the left and the right, each of which is further divided into lobes. Each division of the brain performs certain functions of our everyday living. Discuss the areas of the brain and the functions of each.

2.  The frontal association area of the brain appears to comprise the core of our personalities. Why does this appear to be so? Discuss Phineas Gage's accident in relation to personality changes when this area is damaged.

3.  One hemisphere of our brain is the dominant one. Left-hemisphere dominant means the person is right-handed. Which is dominant with left-handed people? What is meant by a person being ambidextrous?

4.  What comprises the lower brain? Name and discuss the function of each component of the lower brain.

5.  If a person's behavior could be changed chemically in any way you choose, what changes would you make? Why?

6.  The reticular activating system has to do with the alertness of the body. When it is severely damaged the person goes into a deep coma. Stimulation in one area will put an animal to sleep, while stimulation in another area will arouse the animal. Suppose this structure could be altered so that we never had to sleep. What would be the advantages? The disadvantages?

7.  Explain in detail how nerve impulses are transmitted.

8.  The brain works in conjunction with the endocrine system to make our bodies function more efficiently. Explain the endocrine system and its functions.

9.  Television and movies erroneously depict many situations involving brain control. How much truth is there to this? Fully explain.

10. Discuss in detail the central nervous system, the peripheral nervous system, and the somatic nervous system.

## ACTIVITIES

1. A malfunction of the pituitary gland could result in what is called giantism. An insufficient secretion of the thyroid gland could result in cretinism. Research some abnormalities resulting from faulty glandular functions and write up a report to present to the class.

2. Polygraph testing is a fascinating topic, and results of such tests are sometimes hotly debated. The polygraph registers slight changes in body functions which may occur when the person is not telling the truth, hence its popular name, the lie detector. Invite someone to speak to the class on the use and effectiveness of polygraph testing. Perhaps he/she could demonstrate how it is used. Do some research in advance of the visit so that you may benefit more fully from the presentation.

3. Another topic of considerable interest is split brain surgery, wherein the two hemispheres are separated, and then each functions almost like an independent brain. Some research has shown that in some such cases one side literally does not know what the other is doing. Research this topic and present your findings to the class.

4. Electroshock therapy is another topic which should provide much interesting information. Research this subject and, if possible, interview someone in a mental hospital or other mental health facility. Questions you may want to ask would include: How extensively is electroshock therapy used today? How extensively was it used in the past? How did it effect the person? What are the immediate effects? What are the long term effects? For what purpose is it used today? For what purpose was it used in the past? Are there alternate procedures which may be more beneficial to the patient?

5. As a matter of interest in relation to brain control, read *Terminal Man* by Michael Crichton, and *Brain* and *Coma* by Robin Cook. Write a report on each, or give an oral presentation to the class.

# Chapter 4    Sensation and Perception

● ● ● ● ● ● ● ● ● ● ● ● ● ● ● ● ● ● ● ● ● ● ● ● ● ● ● ● ● ● ● ● ● ● ● ● ●

## VOCABULARY

**MATCHING:** Choose the appropriate vocabulary word and place the letter in the space provided.

| | | | |
|---|---|---|---|
| a. | sensation | w. | Mueller-Lyer Illusion |
| b. | perception | x. | pitch |
| c. | white light | y. | intensity |
| d. | cornea | z. | decibels |
| e. | lens | aa. | eardrum |
| f. | pupil | bb. | cochlea |
| g. | retina | cc. | auditory nerve |
| h. | blind spot | dd. | cutaneous receptors |
| i. | absolute threshold | ee. | olfaction |
| j. | cone | ff. | cilia |
| k. | afterimage | gg. | olfactory bulbs |
| l. | audition | hh. | adaptation |
| m. | color constancy | ii. | size constancy |
| n. | brightness constancy | jj. | reversible figure |
| o. | space constancy | kk. | subliminal perception |
| p. | depth perception | ll. | gestalt |
| q. | visual cliff | mm. | iris |
| r. | retinal disparity | nn. | proximity |
| s. | gradient texture | oo. | hair cells |
| t. | similarity | pp. | color blindness |
| u. | closure | qq. | timbre |
| v. | illusion | rr. | taste receptors |
| | | ss. | shape constancy |

_____ 1. The opening in the eye

_____ 2. An apparatus used to demonstrate depth perception

_____ 3. Piece of skin stretched over the entrance to the ear; vibrates to sound

_____ 4. Hair-like extensions on cells; in the nose, they act as receptors to receive odor molecules

_____ 5. Organized whole, shape, or form

_____ 6. The level of sensory stimulation necessary for sensation to occur.

_____ 7. The process of receiving information from the environment

_____ 8. The ability to perceive an object the same color regardless of the environment

_____ 9. How high or low a sound is

_____ 10. Perceptual cue that involves grouping like things together

_____ 11. Image that remains after stimulation of the retina has ended.

_____ 12. The ability to keep an object's brightness constant as the object is moved to various environments

_____ 13. How loud a sound is

_____ 14. Units that receive odor molecules and communicate with the brain regarding them

_____ 15. The difference between the images provided by the two retinas. When the images are brought together in the brain, they provide a sense of depth.

_____ 16. Light as it originates from the sun or a bulb before it is broken up into different frequencies

_____ 17. Stimulation presented below the level of consciousness

_____ 18. The process of organizing sensory information to make it meaningful

_____ 19. Inaccurate perception

_____ 20. The gradual loss of attention to unwanted sensory information

_____ 21. Bundle of nerves carrying sound to the brain

_____ 22. Clear outer covering of the eye behind which is a fluid

_____ 23. A snail-shaped unit filled with fluid and lined with special cells

_____ 24. Keeping objects in the environment steady by perceiving either ourselves or outside objects as moving

_____ 25. Sense of hearing

_____ 26. Illusion in which one line in a picture seems longer than the other but really isn't

_____ 27. Skin; touch

_____ 28. The ability to retain the size of an object regardless of where it is located

_____ 29. Portion of the retina through which the optic nerves exit

_____ 30. The part of the eye that focuses an image on the retina

_____ 31. Illusion in which two alternate figures are seen, first one then the other

_____ 32. A measure of how loud a sound is, its intensity

_____ 33. Receptor that responds during daylight; receives color

_____ 34. The sense of smell

_____ 35. A perceptual cue that involves grouping together things that are near one another

_____ 36. The back of the eye which contains millions of receptors for light

_____ 37. How rough or smooth objects appear; used in depth perception

_____ 38. The ability to see the relation of objects in space

_____ 39. Filling in the missing details of what is viewed

_____ 40. Controls the amount of light coming into the eye

_____ 41. Receptor cells for hearing found in the cochlea

_____ 42. The complexity of a sound

_____ 43. Chemical receptors that decode molecules of food or drink to identify them

_____ 44. Inability to tell the difference between certain colors

_____ 45. The ability to perceive an object as having the same shape regardless of the angle

# REVIEW/TEST PREPARATION

**COMPLETION:** Write the missing word(s) in the blank.

1.  The process of receiving information from the environment is known as _____. Our interpretation of the incoming messages is _____.

2.  Light starts from the sun or a light bulb as _____. We see color because of different _____.

3.  The eye is composed of a _____, a clear outer covering behind which is a fluid; the _____, which controls the amount of incoming light; the _____ which helps us focus; the _____, which expands and contracts and is located in the center of the iris; and the _____, the photosensitive surface of the eye which acts like the film in a camera. The place where the optic nerve leaves the eye is called the _____. The retina is made up of two different kinds of receptors, _____, and _____. The receptors used for night vision are _____, and those used in the day time or for color are _____. All the colors we see are _____, _____, and _____, or a mixture of these three.

4.  A person who does not see certain colors is called _____. The most common form of this is found in those who can see _____ areas, but not _____ ones. People who have none of their cone system working and who see only with their rods are truly _____, but these people are very rare.

5.  When you stare at a colored object for a minute or so, look away from the object and stare at a white piece of paper you will see the object in opposite colors. This is an _____ _____.

6.  In hearing, or _____, the energy form is sound waves. Different sounds vary in _____, or how high or low the sound is and in _____, which measures sound complexity. Sounds also vary in _____, how loud they are. This is measured in _____.

7. The cupped design of the outer ear catches sound waves and sends them toward the

   _____, which vibrates and causes a small bone to vibrate. This causes a

   second bone to also vibrate. The third bone is attached to a snail-shaped structure called the

   _____ which is filled with fluid and small hairs. The key to hearing is the

   20,000 _____. The electrical impulse from the nerve cell connected to

   each of these goes through the _____ to the brain, where the

   sound pattern is interpreted.

8. There are three types of skin, or _____ receptors. The first registers the

   lightest touch, the second responds to change in temperature, and the third is continuously

   active to injury or poison.

9. The sense of smell, or _____, depends on chemical detection to work.

   Inside the nasal cavity are microscopic hairs called _____, which, when the odor

   molecules attach to them, send an electrical signal to the _____.

   These send a code to the brain for interpretation.

10. Animals use smell to communicate sexual interest. The body sends out chemicals called

    _____ to attract a possible partner.

11. Taste receptors operate by chemical communication. These are red spots on the tongue

    called _____. There are four types of receptors: _____,

    _____, _____, and _____.

12. When we interpret and organize sensations to make our world make sense, this is called

    _____. We hold things steady or constant to make sense of our

    environment. The constancies we use are _____, _____,

    _____, and _____.

13. The ability to see objects in space is _____. The difference

    between the images received by each of our eyes is known as _____

    _____.

14. The amount of detail we can distinguish is called _____,

    or how clear the details of objects are. Other perceptual cues are _____

    and _____.

15. An _____ is when we perceive something inaccurately.

16. Stimulation presented below the level of consciousness is known as_____

    _____. Receiving information without the aid of the known senses is called

    _____.

# WORKSHEET

**DIRECTIONS:** Label the parts of the eye and ear below.

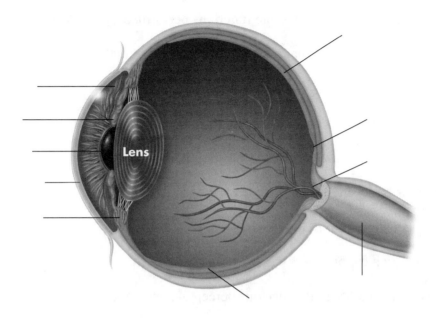

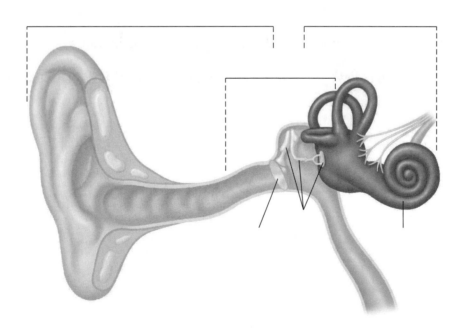

Name _____ Date _____ Period _____

## DISCUSSION

1. In what ways are sensation and perception the same? How do they differ? Explain each.

2. Describe the structure of the eye and the functions performed by each part.

3. Fully explain color blindness. What makes a person color blind?

4. Explain afterimages.

5. The stimulus for hearing is sound waves which enter the outer ear and go through the inner mechanisms of the ear. Name and describe these parts and how sound travels to the brain. Also, name the physical characteristics of these sound waves.

6. What are the four basic smells?

7. What are cutaneous receptors? How do they work?

8. How do sounds reach the brain?

9. Describe the constancies that influence our perceptual accuracy.

10. What is retinal disparity? Explain.

11. Explain each of these perceptual cues: similarity and closure.

12. What are illusions? How do we react to them?

13. How may subliminal perception effect the individual? Discuss its value or lack of value.

14. What is ESP? Do you believe you possess any of these forms of ESP? Discuss.

Name _____ Date _____ Period _____

## ACTIVITIES

1.  Ask your teacher if you may bring an abstract painting to class. You may secure a copy from magazines, or a copy from an art supply store, or make your own by cutting random pieces of construction paper and gluing them to a sheet of paper. Show this to your classmates and ask them to describe what it makes them think of. Be sure that they understand that this is *not* a projective test. Tell your classmates that the physical stimulus is the same for everybody, but each will react to the picture according to how he or she perceives it. How would a physicist describe the picture? Why? Tell the class that psychologists study the reasons why we react differently to the same physical stimulus.

2.  Take a prism to class and put it in the path of a ray of sunlight. The white light will separate into the component colors of red, orange, yellow, green, blue, indigo, and violet. The mnemonic device for remembering the colors is Roy G. Biv. If you have a second prism you may invert it and pass the separated light waves through it, causing them to return to the white light source. An easy activity, almost like magic!

3.  Hold a pen or pencil straight up in either of your hands. Close one eye (either one) and line the pencil up with a corner of the classroom (or any room). Now alternately open and close each eye. The pen or pencil appears to move from left to right. You have just demonstrated binocular disparity.

4.  Make a set of ESP cards. A set consists of five each of a cross, a star, a circle, a square, and wavy lines. You should have a total of 25 cards. Arrange with the teacher to conduct this ESP experiment. Have two classmates who think they have ESP sit with their desks back to back. Shuffle the cards and have one of these students hold the cards and "send messages" as to which card he or she is looking at. The other student, the subject, writes on a sheet of paper the shape on the card which he or she perceives. Tally the number of correct guesses. If the subject exceeds the number one would get by chance, then he/she may be presumed to have ESP. You may wish to reshuffle the cards and repeat the experiment. Watch for things which may be interpreted as signals between the two players. A variation may be to have one student "send" the messages and several (or even the whole class!) receive the messages and record them. Again, tally each to see if any of your classmates may possibly have ESP!

# Chapter 5    *Motivation and Emotion*

● ● ● ● ● ● ● ● ● ● ● ● ● ● ● ● ● ● ● ● ● ● ● ● ● ● ● ● ● ● ● ● ● ●

## VOCABULARY

**DIRECTIONS:** Write the correct term in the blank space.

1. The drive to seek a goal, such as food, water, or friends

   _____

2. Sex glands that make sperm or eggs for reproduction

   _____

3. Another name for sugar in the blood

   _____

4. Forces that push an organism into action to reach a goal

   _____

5. Theory of emotion which says that first the body responds, then one feels the emotion

   _____

6. Needs at the bottom of Maslow's hierarchy; hunger and thirst

   _____

7. The alertness control center of the brain that regulates activity level of the body

   _____

8. Motivation that comes from within the individual

   _____

9. The satisfaction obtained from pleasant, soft physical stimulation

   _____

10. System which ranks human needs one above the other with the most basic needs for physical survival at the bottom of the pyramid; proposed by the psychologist Abraham Maslow

    _____

11. Bodily process of maintaining a balanced internal state

_____

12. A drive that moves one to handle and use objects in the environment

_____

13. Male hormones; they control sexual interest in both males and females

_____

14. Part of the inner brain that controls basic needs and desires: pleasure, pain, fear, rage, hunger, thirst, and sex

_____

15. Theory of emotion proposed by Stanley Schachter which holds that people label a bodily response by giving it the name of the emotion they think they are feeling

_____

16. A drive that moves one to see new and different things

_____

17. Psychological need to belong to and identify with groups

_____

18. Needs at the fourth level of Maslow's hierarchy: liking and respecting yourself, feeling important and useful

_____

19. Glands that cause excitement in order to prepare the body for an emergency or for some important activity

_____

20. State of the body causing feelings such as hope, fear, or love

_____

21. Symbolic thought processes

_____

22. Needs at the second level of Maslow's hierarchy; shelter, nest egg of money

_____

23. Amount of sugar (glucose) contained in the blood which indicates the level of hunger

_____

24. Gland that controls other glands and hormones, as well as producing its own hormone that regulates growth

_____

25. The theory which says that the bodily reaction and the emotional response occur at the same time

_____

26. Needs at top of the hierarchy; establishing meaningful goals and a purpose in life

_____

27. Needs at the third level of Maslow's hierarchy; friendship, closeness with another

_____

28. Motivation that comes from outside the individual

_____

29. The female sex hormone

_____

30. Body regulating mechanism that determines a person's typical weight

_____

31. Female sex gland; makes eggs

_____

32. Male sex glands; make sperm

_____

33. Psychological need to have other people think highly of oneself

_____

34. Psychological need for personal accomplishment

_____

## REVIEW/TEST PREPARATION

**TRUE/FALSE:** Write **T** if the statement is true or **F** if the statement is false.

_____ 1. Motivation is the process of seeking a specific goal.

_____ 2. Emotion is a state of the body which causes feelings.

_____ 3. Centers for both pain and pleasure are located in the thalamus.

_____ 4. The reticular formation controls how high or how low the level of bodily activation is.

_____ 5. The controller of chemical responses are the adrenal glands.

_____ 6. The adrenal glands are located just below the hypothalamus.

_____ 7. The gonads are the sex glands; testes in males, and ovaries in females.

_____ 8. Androgens are the male hormones; estrogen is the female hormone.

_____ 9. A drive results from a bodily need.

_____ 10. Blood-sugar level means that there is an excessive amount of sugar in the blood.

_____ 11. A set point is the body's regulating mechanism governing weight.

_____ 12. Thirst is a result of learning.

_____ 13. A need which we have that is not critical to survival is the need for change.

_____ 14. Humans and a few lower animals also have a curiosity motive.

_____ 15. Manipulation motives are found only in humans.

_____ 16. Intrinsic motivation comes from inside the organism; extrinsic motivation comes from outside the organism.

_____ 17. All animals have a need for physical stimulation, called contact comfort need.

_____ 18. B. F. Skinner developed a theory about a hierarchy of needs.

_____ 19. Emotions are not necessary for our physical well being.

_____ 20. The James-Lange theory of emotion says that first we feel an emotion and then we react.

_____ 21. The Cannon-Bard theory claims that both the bodily reaction and the emotional system respond simultaneously.

_____ 22. The cognitive theory states that emotions come from our labeling them.

_____ 23. The hypothalamus is the controller of other glands.

_____ 24. Adrenaline is another name for sugar in the blood.

_____ 25. It is safe to take drugs to lose weight.

Name _____ Date _____ Period _____

___

# WORKSHEET

___

**DIRECTIONS:** Circle the words listed below in the wordsearch puzzle, and then fill in the blanks with the correct words. The words may be backward, forward, diagonal, or upside down.

cognition
estrogen
set point
androgens
self-esteem
gonads
glucose
testes

motivation
emotion
adrenal glands
pituitary gland
ovaries
hypothalamus
blood-sugar level
manipulation motive
self-actualization

```
A  S  O  V  R  E  N  A  I  X  E  R  O  N  A  S
S  E  L  F  E  S  T  E  E  M  M  O  G  O  N  E
S  I  M  I  M  O  T  I  V  A  T  I  O  N  E  L
I  M  O  T  O  I  V  E  L  D  E  V  N  B  V  F
M  O  T  I  T  G  E  S  T  R  E  S  A  L  I  A
I  M  I  L  I  L  T  A  R  E  T  I  D  O  T  C
A  N  O  R  O  U  E  X  D  N  I  A  S  O  O  T
N  O  N  S  N  C  S  E  N  A  S  E  S  D  M  U
D  H  H  Y  P  O  T  H  A  L  A  M  U  S  N  A
R  O  G  E  N  S  E  E  L  G  L  A  N  U  O  L
O  V  A  R  I  E  S  V  G  L  A  S  T  G  I  I
G  O  N  I  A  D  S  O  Y  A  R  I  E  A  T  Z
E  S  T  E  R  O  G  N  R  N  E  N  G  R  A  A
N  D  R  S  O  G  E  N  A  D  R  E  N  L  L  T
S  E  T  P  O  G  N  T  T  S  E  T  S  E  U  I
B  U  L  I  O  B  U  L  I  M  I  A  M  V  P  O
C  O  G  R  N  I  T  I  U  V  E  B  U  E  I  N
S  E  T  P  O  I  N  T  T  H  Y  P  O  L  N  A
E  S  T  R  N  O  I  T  I  N  G  O  C  G  A  N
E  S  O  C  G  L  U  C  P  O  G  N  I  T  M  A
```

1. Female hormone _____

2. Mechanism which determines one's ideal weight _____

3. Feelings such as hope, fear, love, etc. _____

4. Part of the inner brain that controls basic needs and desires _____

5.   Feeling important and useful _____

6.   Symbolic thought process _____

7.   Another name for sugar in the blood _____

8.   Amount of sugar in the blood; indicates level of hunger _____

9.   Drive which moves us to handle and use objects in the environment

     _____

10.  Sex glands _____

11.  Female sex glands _____

12.  The process of seeking a goal _____

13.  Secrete adrenaline_____

14.  Male sex glands _____

15.  Hormones that control male and female sexual interests _____

16.  Establishing meaningful and purposeful goals in life _____

17.  Controller of other glands; secretes growth hormone _____

# DISCUSSION

1. Motivation is a very important and useful concept. Why?

2. How does motivation affect your body?

3. Name the factors which may make you hungry. Which parts of your nervous system are involved?

4. What are several factors which may make you thirsty?

5. Explain the relationship of hormones to the sex drive. Is the sex drive the same for humans and animals? Explain.

6. How do physiological and learned motives differ in the way they affect us?

7. Explain Maslow's hierarchy of needs.

8. What is an emotion?

9. Three major theories of emotion are discussed in the text. Compare and contrast these theories. How do they differ? How do they agree?

10. Are emotions learned or innate? Why? Back up your answer from material in the text.

11. What is meant by set points?

12. Why is taking drugs for weight control *not* a very wise decision?

## ACTIVITIES

1. All of us watch TV, listen to the radio, and look at magazines. All three forms of media depend on advertising for money, and advertisers are trying to sell their products to make money. The ads are formulated to motivate consumers to buy the products. HOW do they try to get people to buy their product to satisfy a motive? As you watch TV, listen to the radio, and read magazines, take notes on the ads and commercials. Then, from your notes, decide to which motive the advertiser was directing the appeal. Show this on the chart below.

Which motives were appealed to in the ads? How?

| MOTIVE | TV | RADIO | MAGAZINES |
|--------|-----|-------|-----------|
|        |     |       |           |
|        |     |       |           |
|        |     |       |           |
|        |     |       |           |
|        |     |       |           |

2. These days many high school students have part-time jobs. Make a list of ten reasons why you work. If you do not work, write ten reasons why you would like to work. Now rank your reasons, 1 being the primary reason you work, through 10, being the least important reason why you work. Examine your list and the rankings and answer the following questions.

   (a) Are you working primarily just for money? _____

   Why? _____

   (b) Does your work interfere with your school work? _____

   How? _____

   (c) If you could choose not to work, would you? _____

   Why or why not? _____

   (d) Is your work related to a career choice? _____

   How? _____

3. We are intrinsically or extrinsically motivated to perform certain tasks. Rate the following with an *I* if it is intrinsically motivated, and an *E* if it is extrinsically motivated.

   _____ Reading a good book for pleasure

   _____ Doing math homework

   _____ Cleaning my room

   _____ Dressing like my friends

   _____ Driving a certain kind of car

   _____ Going to *the* popular hangout

   _____ In a restaurant, ordering what I like

   _____ Smoking because my friends do it

   _____ Drinking with friends even though I do not like it

   _____ Making good grades

   _____ Staying at home because the party is not the kind I want to attend

   _____ Doing volunteer work after school

   How much of your behavior is intrinsically motivated?

   _____

   How much of your behavior is extrinsically motivated?

   _____

   How could you change this, if you wished to?

   _____

4.  Each of us behaves differently, even when experiencing the same emotions. After each emotion listed, describe your behavior.

anger _____

loneliness _____

fear _____

boredom _____

happiness _____

elation _____

frustration _____

love _____

sadness _____

depression _____

   (a)  What factors cause you to behave as you do?

   _____

   _____

   (b)  What learning is involved in each?

   _____

   _____

   (c)  Which behaviors would you like to change and why?

   _____

   _____

# Chapter 6    *States of Consciousness*

## VOCABULARY

**DIRECTIONS:** Write the correct term on the line below each definition.

1.  Increase in the number of dreams after being deprived of REM sleep

    _____

2.  Sequences of behavioral changes that occur every 24 hours

    _____

3.  Process of reliving one's very early childhood under hypnosis

    _____

4.  Disorder in which one falls instantly into sleep no matter what is going on in the environment

    _____

5.  The organism's awareness of or possibility of knowing what is happening inside or outside itsclf

    _____

6.  Relaxed state just before we fall asleep

    _____

7.  Rapid eye movement sleep; dreams occur during this time

    _____

8.  A horrible dream occurring during NREM when the body is not prepared for it; also called an incubus attack

    _____

9.  Internal chemical units that control regular cycles in parts of the body

    _____

10. Rapid eye movement sleep when we dream

    _____

11. Condition in which a person's breathing often stops while the person is asleep, waking the person

_____

12. A form of self control in which the outside world is cut off from consciousness

_____

13. A concept requiring a belief in something that cannot be seen or touched, but that seems to exist

_____

14. Frightening dream that occurs during REM

_____

15. Cycles set up by biological clocks that are under their own control, ignoring the environment

_____

16. Consciousness just below our present awareness

_____

17. A state of relaxation in which attention is focused on certain objects, acts, or feelings

_____

18. Stage one, fairly relaxed brain waves that occur just before going to sleep

_____

19. Another word for the state of deep relaxation that can occur during hypnosis

_____

20. Thoughts or desires about which we have no direct knowledge

_____

21. The process of altering the free-running cycle to fit a different rhythm

_____

22. Inability to get enough sleep

_____

23. Sleep involving partial thoughts, images or stories, that are poorly organized

_____

24. Rapid brain waves; appear when the person is awake

_____

25. Slow, lazy, deep-sleep brain waves

_____

# REVIEW/TEST PREPARATION

**A. MULTIPLE CHOICE:** Write the letter of the correct answer in the space provided.

_____ 1. A belief in something that cannot be seen or touched, but which appears to be actually present is
   a. consciousness.
   b. a construct.
   c. a conscience.
   d. unconscious.

_____ 2. An awareness of, or the possibility of knowing, what is going on inside or outside of an organism is known as
   a. a conscience.
   b. entrainment.
   c. consciousness.
   d. a construct.

_____ 3. When a forbidden word is flashed on a screen, the brain responds electrically even when people claim not to have seen it. It is registered in the
   a. unconscious.
   b. subconscious.
   c. conscious.
   d. conscience.

_____ 4. The level of consciousness which contains thoughts and desires we are unaware of is the
   a. unconscious.
   b. subconscious.
   c. conscience.
   d. preconscious.

_____ 5. Rapid brain waves which appear when a person is awake.
   a. delta waves
   b. alpha waves
   c. omega waves
   d. beta waves

_____ 6. Internal chemical units that control regular cycles in parts of the body are
   a. biological forces.
   b. chronobiology.
   c. chronometers.
   d. biological clocks.

_____ 7. The process of altering the free-running cycle of biological clocks to fit a different rhythm is called
   a. entrainment.
   b. socialization.
   c. hypnosis.
   d. sociobiological.

_____ 8. Behavioral changes that occur every twenty-four hours are operating on
   a. biological time clocks.
   b. circadian rhythms.
   c. consciousness levels.
   d. biorhythms.

_____ 9. One of the most important reasons we sleep is that we must have
   a. rest.
   b. NREM time.
   c. dreams.
   d. quiet time.

_____ 10. Paradoxically, dreams occur in a stage of light sleep, during a time when it is very difficult to awaken the sleeper. This is known as
   a. REM sleep.
   b. twilight sleep.
   c. NREM sleep.
   d. delta wave sleep.

_____ 11. Dreams actually last
   a. only seconds.
   b. 5 to 40 minutes.
   c. several hours.
   d. 2 to 3 minutes.

_____ 12. Brain waves in the deepest sleep stage are called
   a. alpha waves.
   b. delta waves.
   c. beta waves.
   d. beta blockers.

_____ 13. A frightening dream, a nightmare, may occur if REM sleep is blocked for a period of time. This is known as
   a. NREM sleep.
   b. delta wave blockage.
   c. REM rebound.
   d. deep sleep syndrome.

_____ 14. An incubus attack, or really horrible nightmare, occurs during
   a. twilight sleep.
   b. REM sleep.
   c. deep sleep.
   d. NREM sleep.

_____ 15. What percent of our dreams are in color, what percent in black and white?
   a. 75 percent color; 25 percent black and white
   b. 33 percent color; 67 percent black and white
   c. 50 percent color; 50 percent black and white
   d. 40 percent color; 60 percent black and white

_____ 16. Sleepwalking or talking occurs during
      a. deep REM sleep.
      b. deep NREM sleep.
      c. the first REM sleep of the night.
      d. the "twilight" stage.

_____ 17. When one has trouble sleeping, he or she is said to have
      a. narcolepsy.
      b. sleep apnea.
      c. insomnia.
      d. nightmares.

_____ 18. The problem that occurs when a person goes into instant REM sleep anywhere, anytime, is called
      a. narcolepsy.
      b. sleep apnea.
      c. insomnia.
      d. amnesia.

_____ 19. Older people may suffer from a condition in which they stop breathing many times during sleep, called
      a. sleep apnea.
      b. narcolepsy.
      c. amnesia.
      d. insomnia.

_____ 20. The state in which attention is focused on certain objects, acts, or feelings is known as
      a. suggestiveness.
      b. hypnosis.
      c. narcolepsy.
      d. focal point.

_____ 21. A trance is a state of
      a. fortunetelling.
      b. prophecy.
      c. relaxation.
      d. clairvoyance.

_____ 22. A form of self control wherein all outside interference is shut out by focusing on a steady sound or rhythm is
      a. REM sleep.
      b. hypnotism.
      c. narcolepsy.
      d. meditation.

**B. TRUE/FALSE:** Write **T** if the statement is true or **F** if the statement if false.

_____ 23. Hypnosis is of some practical use.

_____ 24. Meditation is very bad because it alters brain waves.

_____ 25. A trance is a state of deep relaxation.

_____ 26. A hypnotist can make people do anything through posthypnotic suggestion.

Name _____ Date _____ Period _____

## WORKSHEET

**COMPLETION:** Write your answers to the following.

1. (a) What are the effects of hypnosis in regard to the following?

   smoking _____

   weight loss _____

   drinking _____

   minor pain _____

   childbirth _____

   headaches _____

   memory _____

   (b) What are the effects of meditation in regard to biological functions?

   _____

   _____

2. Two kinds of sleep are REM and NREM. Describe each.

   REM _____

   _____

   NREM _____

   _____

3. The typical sleep cycle and brain changes during sleep are as follows:

   (a) Before sleep, when we are awake: _____ waves. We get into bed and

   relax, stage 1: _____ waves.

   (b) stage 2 (twilight stage): _____

   (c) stage 3: _____

   (d) stage 4: _____ waves.

   (e) After reaching stage 4, we head back to stage _____. However, instead of

   regular stage _____, we enter _____, which is

   _____.

(f) The second type of sleep is _____, during which the brain is

   still active, providing _____.

## DISCUSSION

1.  Explain consciousness.

2.  Two levels of consciousness are subconscious and unconscious. Explain each.

3.  Explain biological clocks, including what is meant by free-running clocks and entrainment.

4.  Every living thing operates on a circadian rhythm. What is meant by this? How does this affect human beings?

5.  Explain what may happen when we behave contrary to our biological clocks.

6.  Explain what happens to people who are awakened each time they enter REM sleep.

7.  Describe the stages of sleep.

8.  Why is REM sleep important?

9.  When do sleepwalking and sleeptalking occur?

10. Explain NREM sleep. Do we dream during this stage?

11. The text describes three major hypotheses for why we dream. Explain each.

12. Humans have, throughout history, believed dreams to be mystical experiences. What is your explanation of dreams? What does the text say about dream content? How does this differ from what you think?

13. Discuss any nightmares you have had. What do you think caused them?

14. Generally speaking, teenagers "live" for weekends. Explain how too much social entrainment of sleep cycles may affect them.

15. What are some effects which may be gained through meditation?

## ACTIVITIES

1.  Sigmund Freud wrote several books on dreams, dream content, and dream interpretation. Research what he wrote, plus the writings of several other authors on the subject of dreams. Compare and contrast what they have to say. Write a report to present to the class. Do you have your own theory about dreams? If so, include that in your report.

2.  Most dreams occur during REM sleep, which occurs on an average of every 90 minutes. Everybody dreams, though there are those who say they do not. This is perhaps because they cannot recall their dreams. This exercise is designed to help you become more aware of your dreams and how often you dream.

    (a) As you prepare for bed, put a pencil and pad, and a clock on a table or nightstand next to your bed.

    (b) Make a note of the time just before you drift off to sleep.

    (c) While asleep, try to become aware that you are dreaming. With practice you should be able to learn this.

    (d) When you have learned to become aware that you are dreaming, try to wake up. REM sleep is a light sleep, but the sleeper is hard to wake up. However, if you practice, you will be able to accomplish it.

    (e) When you have succeeded in waking yourself, write down the time and what you were dreaming about. In your dreams you will have characters acting out a plot in a certain setting, usually displaying some emotions. Are your dreams in color?

    (f) Record the time again each morning when you awaken.

    (g) Do this for seven succeeding nights and then record the information on the following Dream Scheme.

Name _____ Date _____ Period _____

## DREAM SCHEME

| | Amt. of Sleep | Setting | Plot | Characters | Emotions | Colors |
|---|---|---|---|---|---|---|
| Monday | | | | | | |
| Tuesday | | | | | | |
| Wednesday | | | | | | |
| Thursday | | | | | | |
| Friday | | | | | | |
| Saturday | | | | | | |
| Sunday | | | | | | |

Now answer the following:

1. How much did you sleep each night? _____

2. Was there a pattern to your dreaming?

   _____

3. Were there recurring themes or plots in your dreams? _____

   If so, what? _____

4. Was there anything in your dreams that you could relate to your reality a day or several
   days earlier? If so, explain

   _____

   _____

5. The text gives three major hypotheses for why we dream. Can you relate one or more of
   these to your dreams?

   _____

   _____

   _____

6. Did you dream more during the week or on the weekend? How do you explain this?

   _____

   _____

   _____

# Chapter 7    Principles of Learning

● ● ● ● ● ● ● ● ● ● ● ● ● ● ● ● ● ● ● ● ● ● ● ● ● ● ● ● ● ● ● ● ● ● ● ●

## VOCABULARY

**DIRECTIONS:** Fill in the blanks with the correct term.

| | |
|---|---|
| conditioning | generalization |
| classical conditioning | discrimination learning |
| stimulus | shaping |
| response | chaining |
| unconditioned stimulus | schedules of reinforcement |
| unconditioned response | continuous reinforcement |
| conditioned stimulus | partial reinforcement schedule |
| conditioned response | variable ratio schedule |
| stimulus generalization | fixed ratio schedule |
| extinction | variable interval schedule |
| operant conditioning | fixed interval schedule |
| reinforcement | social learning |
| primary reinforcement | observational learning |
| secondary reinforcement | cognitive approach |
| positive reinforcement | cognitive map |
| negative reinforcement | strategies |
| punishment | |

1.   Method of conditioning in which associations are made between a natural stimulus and a
     learned, neutral stimulus. _____

2.   The stimulus which automatically elicits a response is called _____,
     and the automatic response is called _____.

3.   Previously neutral stimulus that has been associated with a natural stimulus is called the
     _____, and the response is known as the _____
     _____.

4.   Process in which a response spreads from one specific stimulus to other stimuli that
     resemble the original _____.

5.   Learning to tell the difference between one event or object and another, the reverse of
     generalization, is called _____.

6.  The gradual loss of an association over time is known as _____.

7.  Conditioning that results from the individual's actions and the consequences they cause is known as _____.

8.  A _____ is something that is absolutely essential for survival, such as food, water, etc.

9.  The reinforcer necessary for psychological or physical survival that is used as a reward is called a_____.

10. _____ strengthens a response because it is presented or given to the animal.

11. _____ strengthens the response because it is stopped or removed.

12. _____ is designed to stop or weaken a response by following it with unpleasant consequences.

13. Generally, animals who perform in a circus learn their tricks by being rewarded in steps leading up to the desired response. This is known as _____.

14. When an animal has learned a number of desired responses, these may be put together to form a sequence of acts. This is known as _____.

15. Different methods of reinforcing, called _____, are used wherein the animal is not reinforced after every response. This is known as _____ _____.

16. The schedule of reinforcement wherein the number of responses varies before reinforcement is given is the _____.

17. When reinforcement is given after a desired act is performed a fixed number of times, we call this the _____.

18. If an organism is given a reinforcement after a desired act occurs following a fixed amount of time, it is on a _____.

19. The schedule in which reinforcement occurs after a desired act is performed following a variable amount of time is called the _____.

20. We learn patterns of behavior by watching others and deciding what to imitate. This behavior is acquired by _____.

21. An approach to the study of learning that emphasizes abstract mental processes and previous knowledge is the _____.

22. A mental images of where one is located in space. These are called _____ _____.

23. In addition to forming cognitive maps, rats in mazes also used techniques for solving problems called _____.

Name _____ Date _____ Period _____

## REVIEW/TEST PREPARATION

**DIRECTIONS:** Briefly answer the following:

1. There are four types of learning. Explain each.

   (a) classical conditioning _____

   _____

   (b) operant conditioning _____

   _____

   (c) social learning _____

   _____

   (d) cognitive approach _____

   _____

2. Explain each of the following terms:

   (a) unconditioned stimulus _____

   _____

   (b) unconditioned response _____

   _____

   (c) conditioned stimulus _____

   _____

   (d) conditioned response _____

   _____

   (e) generalization _____

   _____

   (f) discrimination _____

   _____

   (g) extinction _____

   _____

3. How are classical and operant conditioning different?

_____

_____

_____

4. How are positive and negative reinforcement alike?

_____

_____

_____

5. Differentiate between negative reinforcement and punishment.

_____

_____

_____

6. Explain primary reinforcement and secondary reinforcement.

_____

_____

_____

7. Shaping and chaining are used extensively in training animals. How is this done with training Seeing Eye dogs?

_____

_____

_____

8. There are four partial reinforcement schedules. Which schedule is used in each of the following?

   (a) Gambler _____

   (b) Migrant worker paid by the bushel for crop picked _____

   (c) Nurse who is paid every two weeks _____

   (d) Fisherman _____

9.  How does learning occur, according to the social learning theory?

    _____

    _____

    _____

10. How may one be helped to overcome an irrational fear (phobia)?

    _____

    _____

    _____

11. Explain the terms *cognitive map* and *strategies*.

    _____

    _____

    _____

# WORKSHEET

## WHO/WHAT AM I?

1.  I am the process whereby animals are taught a complicated response by being rewarded in steps leading up to the response.

    What am I? _____

2.  I am an approach to the study of learning that emphasizes mental processes and previous knowledge.

    What am I? _____

3.  In my laboratory research using dogs as subjects I accidentally discovered the process of classical conditioning.

    Who am I? _____

4.  I am the mental image of where one is located in space.

    What am I? _____

5.  I am the result of making an association between an event and something positive or negative by repeated exposure.

    What am I? _____

6.  My name is almost always closely associated with operant conditioning. I have done extensive research using animals as subjects.

    Who am I? _____

7.  I am the gradual loss of an association over time.

    What am I? _____

8.  I am the name given to all learning in a social situation.

    What am I? _____

9.  I am the event which occurs as a result of presentation of a conditioned stimulus.

    What am I? _____

10. I am the process of weakening a response by following it with unpleasant consequences. Little kids do not like me.

    What am I? _____

# DISCUSSION

1. Classical and operant conditioning are two ways in which people may learn. List some of your own behaviors and try to determine if they may have been acquired through one of these methods of conditioning. Consider the stimuli for each, the response, and any reinforcers or rewards. Were these reinforcers positive or negative? Primary or secondary? Explain how generalization and discrimination may have occurred. Can you remember some things which you did at one time but do not do now? Could this have been extinction? Explain.

2. A phobia is an irrational fear. All of us fear certain things in varying degrees. Make a list of things which you fear. If possible, also list the circumstances related to the time you acquired these fears. How could you go about getting rid of these phobias?

3. B. F. Skinner believed that how we turn out in life is the result of all the operations we make over the years. Consider this carefully. Now, write an argument favoring Skinner's claim. After you have done this, write an argument refuting Skinner's claim. This may be a good class project, half the class writing in favor of Skinner's claim and the other half against it. Present these claims orally and discuss the pros and cons.

4. Albert Bandura believed that a more complex explanation for behavior than the robot-like stimulus-response of the conditioning theorists was needed when analyzing group or social behavior. He is an adherent of the social learning theory. Explain basically what this theory is, and then analyze your own behavior. How much of what you do could be attributed to this type of learning? Explain.

5. Much work about learning today is being done in an area called the cognitive approach. Explain this approach. Do you agree with it? Why or why not?

6. Discuss in detail some of the complexities of conditioning.

7. A cognitive map refers to a human and animal ability to form a mental image of where one is located in the environment. Explain this concept in relation to learning.

8. Make an outline of "Trying to Learn How to Try to Learn." Put this into practice in several of your subject areas. Compare your grades at the end of a three-week period with your previous grades. Was there improvement? What factors may have interfered with your learning? Did you find the method effective? Why or why not?

# ACTIVITIES

1.  Suppose that you wish to teach your dog a new trick. *(If you do not have a dog, pretend that you do!)*
    Set up your experiment, naming the response sought, the method of reinforcement (schedule), and whether this would be positive or negative reinforcement. Would you also incorporate punishment? Why or why not?

2.  Using the same dog (real or imaginary), teach it a more complicated response which would involve shaping. Explain the steps you would take in getting the dog to respond in the desired way. You may wish to teach the dog several responses which you could then chain together. Explain the process you would follow.

3.  All of us perform certain responses over and over, some of which are good, some bad. These are called habits. Make a list of ten of your habits, both good and bad. Beside each habit write down reinforcement(s) for it. Choose one of the habits you listed as bad that you would like to stop or change (such as biting your nails, twisting your hair, etc.). Note the frequency and the conditions under which you engage in this behavior. Try to change these as much as you can. What reinforcement do you receive? Change this, too, if possible. Now decide what reward you would like to receive for getting rid of this habit, set a time limit on yourself, and work toward the elimination or changing of this habit. Each time you are tempted to indulge in the habit, think of the reward. Depending on the habit, how long you have had it, and the time limit and reward you set for yourself, you should be successful within a reasonable time. Do keep the good habits!

4.  Psychology students love to "use psychology" on their teachers, and teachers, whether they know it or not, use psychology on their students. Teachers reinforce behaviors of students, some behaviors good, some bad, but they are reinforced. Make a study of the teacher-student interactions in your classes. Note the behavior of the students and then note the response of the teachers, either word or action. Also note whether the behavior is acceptable classroom behavior ("good") or not acceptable ("bad"). Do the teachers respond in a manner to strengthen the behavior (positive or negative reinforcement), or in a manner to stop the behavior (punishment)? You may also want to note how the teachers' responses affect the class as a whole.

5.  In order not to reinforce every response an organism makes, schedules of reinforcement were devised. The experimenter chooses a schedule of reinforcement in accordance with the type of desired response. Describe the following schedules and tell what kind of response rates and the duration (resistance to extinction) which may be expected.

    (a) fixed ratio _____

    _____

    response rate and duration _____

    _____

(b)  variable ratio _____

_____

response rate and duration _____

_____

(c)  Fixed interval _____

_____

Response rate and duration _____

_____

(d)  Variable interval _____

_____

Response rate and duration _____

_____

6.  You have a little brother or sister who is deathly afraid of white furry animals. Explain the
    procedure you might use to help this child overcome this fear.

_____

_____

_____

_____

_____

_____

_____

_____

_____

_____

_____

7. Read the following two situations and answer the questions below each.
   **Situation I**

   Jane was in the kitchen baking cookies with her three year old daughter Susie. Jane told Susie it was nap time. Susie began fussing, but Jane remained firm and said, "Nap time." Susie began to whine, saying "I don't want to take a nap! I want to make more cookies." Jane weakly insisted on the nap. At that point Susie began to cry, whereupon Jane allowed Susie to stay up to help finish baking the cookies. Susie stopped crying.

   (a) Was Jane's or Susie's behavior positively reinforced?

   _____

   (b) Was Jane's or Susie's behavior negatively reinforced?

   _____

   (c) Name the positive reinforcer.

   _____

   (d) Name the negative reinforcer.

   _____

   (e) Name the positively reinforced response.

   _____

   (f) Name the negatively reinforced response.

   _____

   **Situation II**

   The family dog, Buffy, always positioned herself beside the family at dinner time. She began begging beside Mr. Smith's chair. Being unsuccessful, she moved to Mrs. Smith's chair and then on to Dan's chair. Finally she moved to Pat's chair, begging more intently. Pat, unable to bear the dog's pitiful whines, gave her a bite of meat, which Buffy ate with obvious enjoyment. As the meal progressed, Chris slipped a bite to Buffy from time to time.

   (a) Was Pat's or Buffy's behavior positively reinforced?

   _____

   (b) Was Pat's or Buffy's behavior negatively reinforced?

   _____

(c) Name the positive reinforcer.

_____

(d) Name the negative reinforcer.

_____

(e) Name the positively reinforced response.

_____

(f) Name the negatively reinforced response.

_____

8. Millions and millions of dollars are spent on promoting products through advertising. How effective is advertising? Listed below are some partial advertising slogans. Identify the product associated with each of these, and then add as many other slogans as you can think of. Just how effective is conditioning in advertising?

(a) Double your pleasure, double your fun with _____

(b) A sprinkle a day helps keep odor away. _____

(c) It's the real thing. _____

(d) Reach out and touch someone. _____

(e) Good to the last drop. _____

(f) In the valley of the _____, ho, ho, ho.

(g) Ring around the collar _____

(h) Mountain grown flavor _____

(i) _____, because I'm

worth it!

(j) Because you care enough to send the very best. _____

(k) _____

(l) _____

(m) _____

(n) _____

(o) _____

(p) _____

(q) _____

(r) _____

(s) _____

(t) _____

(u) _____

(v) _____

(w) _____

(x) _____

(y) _____

(z) _____

## Chapter 8

### Acquiring, Processing, and Retaining Information

• • • • • • • • • • • • • • • • • • • • • • • • • • • • • • • • • • • • • • • • •

## VOCABULARY

**DIRECTIONS:** Complete the crossword puzzle.

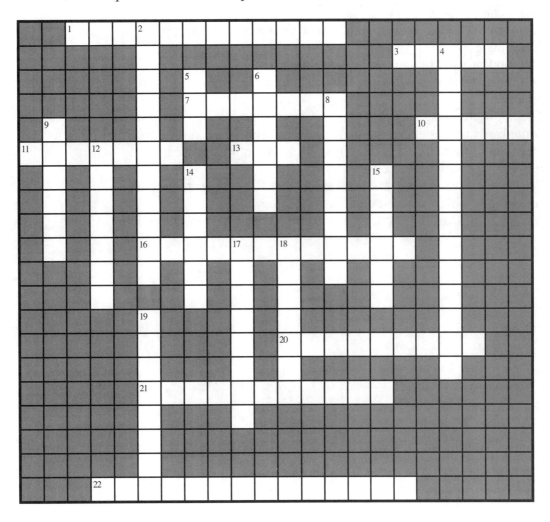

**ACROSS**

1. The idea that we forget because new and old material conflict (interfere) with one another
3. Negative _____fer; interference with learning that results from differences between two tasks
7. Iconic memory lasting a minute or so "in front of the viewer" so objects can be counted or analyzed
10. A gradual upward line representing increased retention of material as the result of learning; learning _____
11. Memory system that includes direct receivers of information from the environment—for example, iconic, acoustic

13. Computer term
16. Learning beyond one perfect recitation so that the forgetting curve will have no effect
20. Memory system that retains information for a few seconds to a few minutes
21. Processing method by which we take in, analyze, store, and retrieve material
22. Unusual associations made to aid memory


**DOWN**
2. The process of attaching a maximum number of associations to an item to be learned so that it can be retrieved more easily
4. Very brief sound memory which can be sent to short-term memory
5. Adult males
6. The total of what one remembers is stored here
8. Putting items into clusters or "chunks" so that the items are learned in groups, rather than separately
9. The ability to bring back and integrate many specific learned details
14. Organized and systematic approach to answering questions or solving problems
17. The type of memory that lasts days, weeks, months, decades
12. Junction between nerve cells
15. Very brief visual memory which can be sent to short-term memory
18. Blocking of older memories and/or loss of new ones
19. A transfer of learning resulting from similarities between two tasks

# REVIEW/TEST PREPARATION

**A. MULTIPLE CHOICE:** Write the letter of the correct answer in the space provided.

_____ 1. Alert focusing on material is
   a. elaboration.
   b. attention.
   c. activity.
   d. positive transfer.

_____ 2. Learning that occurs in one chemical state and is best reproduced when the same state occurs again is called
   a. learning dependency.
   b. faulty learning.
   c. state dependent learning.
   d. material dependency.

_____ 3. A student takes typing for one year. The next year he takes a computer course and finds that the keyboard is easier for him to use than for those students who did not take typing. This is called
   a. positive transfer.
   b. negative transfer.
   c. material transfer.
   d. typing transfer.

_____ 4. Beth learned to drive using her mother's car, which has an automatic transmission. She finds it more difficult to drive her father's car, which has a gear shift. This is an example of
   a. positive transfer.
   b. negative transfer.
   c. transmission trouble.
   d. mechanical transfer.

_____ 5. Information processing refers to the methods by which we
   a. work on computer input.
   b. get information to those who need it.
   c. secure information for a project.
   d. take in, analyze, store, and retrieve information.

_____ 6. Schema comes from the Greek word meaning an outline or pattern. This means that we
   a. have a built-in plan for problem solving.
   b. plot and scheme to get our way.
   c. are able to detect others' schemes.
   d. are able to solve problems without effort.

_____ 7. Which of the following is a mnemonic device?
    a. A rolling stone gathers no moss.
    b. Two wrongs do not equal a right.
    c. Thirty days hath September...
    d. Do unto others...

_____ 8. A method of learning in which an overall view of the matter to be learned is developed so that the material is better organized is known as
    a. focal learning.
    b. principle learning.
    c. segment learning.
    d. serial learning.

_____ 9. Which of the following is an example of chunking?
    a. putting all apples in a separate category
    b. separating all items to be learned
    c. putting things in alphabetical order
    d. putting all trees together to form the concept "tree"

_____ 10. Forgetting means
    a. permanently losing what we have learned.
    b. overlearning.
    c. an increase in errors in bringing back material from memory.
    d. improper learning.

_____ 11. Overlearning is to
    a. spend too much time doing homework.
    b. learn only long enough to take a test.
    c. rehearse over and over beyond one perfect recitation.
    d. learn to the point of sheer boredom.

_____ 12. Memory has been classified into two types:
    a. recall and recognition.
    b. recollection and remembering.
    c. recall and rejection.
    d. recognition and rejuvenation.

_____ 13. Taking an essay test requires using a specialized memory involving
    a. recognition.
    b. recall.
    c. remembering.
    d. rejuvenation.

_____ 14. When you are given a group of old family pictures and asked to identify the relatives, this would involve
    a. recognition.
    b. recall.
    c. remembering.
    d. rejuvenation.

_____ 15. A conflict between the similarity of new material to be stored in memory and material already stored is called
  a. the forgetting curve.
  b. elaboration.
  c. interference.
  d. overlearning.

_____ 16. The major theory to explain forgetting is the
  a. negative transfer theory.
  b. overlearning theory.
  c. information processing theory.
  d. interference theory.

_____ 17. Loss of memory is
  a. amnesia.
  b. schema.
  c. iconic memory.
  d. acoustic memory.

_____ 18. Memory is stored in the following sequence:
  a. STM, iconic or acoustic memory, LTM.
  b. iconic or acoustic memory, STM, LTM.
  c. STM, LTM, iconic or acoustic memory.
  d. acoustic, iconic, LTM, STM.

_____ 19. If you have eidetic imagery, you are said to have a
  a. sensory memory system.
  b. faulty perception memory.
  c. negative transfer of memory.
  d. photographic memory.

_____ 20. Over a period of time memory will solidify until it becomes permanent. This is known as
  a. information processing.
  b. positive transfer.
  c. overlearning.
  d. consolidation.

**B. TRUE/FALSE:** Write **T** if the statement is true or **F** if the statement if false.

_____    1.  Two broad categories of chemicals that influence learning are stimulants and depressants.

_____    2.  Some anxiety about taking a test may serve to stimulate the person.

_____    3.  Any chemical will alter the body's condition or state, thereby making learning impossible.

_____    4.  The most important learning is that centering around survival.

_____    5.  Elaboration is an effective method for storing learned material by using a maximum number of associations.

# WORKSHEET

**DIRECTIONS:** Unscramble the words on the left to find the answer to the statements on the right.

1. mescha

   _____

   The outline or pattern developed by Little Red Riding Hood to answer the question of where her grandmother lives

2. tiotnenta

   _____

   Something you pay (not money) when you are focusing on materials to be learned

3. kignnuch

   _____

   Putting things into clusters so that items are learned in groups, rather than separately

4. gorfingett

   _____

   An increase in errors in bringing material back from memory

5. cmnionem civdee

   _____

   I before e except after c, or when sounded like a as in neighbor and weigh.

6. vearlorennig

   _____

   At first it may sound like studying too much, but it is actually a good way to remember material.

7. clarle

   _____

   When you take an essay test, this is the type of memory you use.

8. coreingiton

   _____

   When you take a multiple choice test, this is the type of memory you use.

9. topisvie

   _____

   If you learn to drive a car with a manual transmission and then drive one with an automatic transmission, this is the kind of transfer you have.

10. inocic

_____

Visual memory you receive very briefly before it is sent to the short-term memory

11. anemias

_____

Someone who receives a severe blow to the head may suffer from this

12. scoutaic

_____

Very brief sound memory which may be sent on to the short-term memory

13. trosh mert

_____

Memory used when you look up a telephone number; Lasts long enough for you to dial

14. dietice

_____

Imagery person has who is said to have a photographic memory

15. givetane

_____

Kind of transfer we experience when what we have learned in the past interferes with the learning of new material

# DISCUSSION

1.  Acquiring information is a highly complex and complicated process. Several factors which may vitally influence this acquiring of information are attention, chemicals, and emotions. Discuss each of these and how they may influence acquisition of knowledge.

2.  A major learning process is called transfer of training. This occurs when prior learning facilitates present learning. This is positive transfer. When prior learning interferes with present learning, it is called negative transfer. Make a list of things which you have learned which helped in later learning. Also, list any prior learning which you found to interfere with later learning.

3.  The text tells us that we have an organized and systematic approach to solving problems, called a schema. In your own words, explain this schema.

4.  Fortunately for us, our brains have the ability to organize information which we take in and store. Write a brief explanation of this.

5.  There are a number of special learning processes which we may use to help us store and retain information. These are the elaboration process, mnemonic devices, principle learning, and chunking. Define each of these processes and tell how you could use each in your own learning process.

6.  Everyone at times will forget something, only to remember what was earlier forgotten at a later time. Forgetting does not necessarily mean that we have lost forever what we have learned. Explain what is meant by this.

7.  Overlearning may sound like someone is studying too hard. But, this is not the case. This is an excellent way to retain information. How would you go about it?

8.  Differentiate between recall and recognition.

9.  It is said that people who have amnesia do not forget everything, that the material that disappears is fairly selective. What is a good explanation for this?

## ACTIVITIES

1. Mnemonic devices are fun while helping us to remember certain, often difficult material. However, they should not be used too often, as there are other and better ways for learning and remembering. Just for fun, ask your parents and other relatives and friends what mnemonic devices they used or still use, and make a collection of them. Do any of these devices represent effective and efficient learning procedures? Are any of them harder to learn than the material they represent?

   Here are several of these devices to get your collection started:

   To remember the names of the planets from the sun outward:

   M VEM J SUN P    (Mercury, Venus, Earth, Mars, Jupiter, Saturn, Uranus, Neptune, Pluto)

   HOMES for the Great Lakes. Can you name them?

2. This activity will require cooperation from your teacher. Arrange for two people (of the same sex or opposite sex) to start a disagreement in the hall outside the door to your classroom just loud enough to attract attention without creating a major disturbance—there are other classrooms to consider. Hopefully these students will be dressed in a fairly nondescript manner and if possible, will not be known to your classmates. After a few seconds have them come into your classroom and create more disruption, again for only a few seconds, then have them run out. After this experience, ask the class to describe what happened. Ask leading questions, such as, "Did you see his/her glasses?" "Did he/she have on a blue, red, green, yellow, or some color, shirt/blouse?" You may have a "stooge" who will deliberately lead the class in giving wrong descriptions. If so, how effective was this? How much did your "eyewitnesses" agree on the event and descriptions of the disrupters?

# Chapter 9    Intelligence and Creativity

· · · · · · · · · · · · · · · · · · · · · · · · · · · · · · · · · · · · · · · ·

---

## VOCABULARY

---

**A.  DIRECTIONS:** Fill in the blank space with the letter of the correct term. Then find the word in the word search on the next page. Words may be horizontal, vertical, diagonal, or backward.

a.  intelligence
b.  group intelligence tests
c.  cultural bias
d.  inclusion
e.  mental age
f.  intelligence quotient
g.  verbal scale

h.  performance scale
i.  picture completion
j.  savant syndrome
k.  creativity
l.  set
m.  break set
n.  mental retardation

_____  1.  IQ test items which try to bypass verbal material and focus on problem solving without words

_____  2.  Come up with unusual unexpected ideas; use something in a way different from the way in which it is normally used

_____  3.  A measure of intelligence obtained by comparing mental age as determined by testing with chronological age

_____  4.  Below average intellectual functioning that prevents a person from being able to perform at the level appropriate for his or her age

_____  5.  IQ test items that rely heavily on word comprehension and usage

_____  6.  A tendency to solve problems in the same way over and over

_____  7.  The ability to understand and adapt to the environment by using a combination of inherited abilities and learning experiences

_____  8.  A test that gives an advantage to a particular group

_____  9.  The practice of keeping children with disabilities in regular academic classrooms

_____  10.  Condition in which a person with below-normal mental capacity possesses a special talent or mental ability to an extremely high degree

_____  11.  IQ tests administered to many people at one time; the tests are highly verbal and use paper and pencil

_____  12.  The level of intellectual functioning in years; compared with chronological age to derive IQ

_____  13.  On the Wechsler test, the test taker is shown pictures from which some important part is missing

_____  14.  Mental processes that result in original, workable ideas

---

| | | | | | | | | | | | | | | | | | | | | |
|---|---|---|---|---|---|---|---|---|---|---|---|---|---|---|---|---|---|---|---|---|
| T | I | N | T | L | L | E | S | B | L | S | C | H | I | O | T | L | E | S | C | A |
| C | O | N | E | A | E | V | E | R | B | A | L | S | C | A | L | E | S | C | A | N |
| I | N | T | T | L | L | I | T | V | E | R | B | S | C | D | A | L | C | C | N | O |
| E | O | A | B | E | R | A | T | I | O | N | Q | E | R | B | L | I | U | T | E | I |
| L | I | T | V | E | L | S | C | A | L | V | R | B | L | P | S | C | L | I | N | T |
| A | S | O | U | T | I | L | E | N | O | I | B | E | C | T | I | O | T | V | B | E |
| C | U | M | P | R | H | S | I | N | C | P | R | E | T | C | T | I | U | N | S | L |
| S | L | S | T | H | O | U | M | G | R | I | S | C | A | B | A | L | R | O | M | P |
| E | C | M | B | R | E | A | K | S | E | T | B | R | K | I | E | A | A | S | E | M |
| C | N | E | T | R | A | K | E | S | S | N | E | T | V | L | I | T | L | B | L | O |
| N | I | N | T | E | L | L | I | G | E | N | C | E | T | I | G | E | B | C | E | C |
| A | T | T | E | N | G | E | N | I | N | C | R | E | A | T | I | V | I | T | Y | E |
| M | E | A | G | E | N | C | E | C | R | E | A | T | Q | Y | I | E | A | B | A | R |
| R | M | L | A | N | C | E | P | E | R | F | S | C | A | U | L | E | S | E | N | U |
| O | L | A | A | C | S | E | C | N | A | C | S | F | R | E | O | P | E | R | U | T |
| F | O | G | N | O | I | T | A | D | R | A | T | E | R | L | A | T | N | E | M | C |
| R | M | E | N | T | R | E | T | A | R | T | I | O | N | M | E | N | I | A | T | I |
| E | M | O | C | E | M | O | R | D | N | Y | S | T | N | A | V | A | S | E | O | P |
| P | R | E | H | E | N | T | E | S | S | A | O | B | J | A | S | E | M | B | N | Y |
| G | R | O | U | P | I | N | T | E | L | L | I | G | E | N | C | E | B | O | N | T |

**B. DIRECTIONS:** Fill in the blank with the correct answer.

1. The original intelligence test, developed by Alfred Binet and refined at Stanford University, is now called the _____.

2. One of four elements on Binet's test, _____ means that the person working on the problem should have some idea whether or not it is correct.

3. _____ are tests which are administered to one person at a time.

4. _____ tests are given to large groups of individuals at the same time.

Name _____ Date _____ Period _____

---

## REVIEW/TEST PREPARATION

---

**DIRECTIONS:** Write your answers to the following in the space provided.

1.  The ability to understand and adapt to the environment by using a combination of inherited abilities and learning experiences is known as _____.

2.  Briefly explain why the first intelligence test was developed, and by whom.

    _____

    _____

    _____

3.  The four elements Binet believed important for intelligence are as follows:

    (a) _____ is the ability to set up a goal and work toward it.

    (b) _____ means that when faced with a problem the person can make the adjustments needed to solve it.

    (c) _____ means having a basic understanding of exactly what the problem is.

    (d) _____ means that the person working on the problem should have some idea regarding whether or not it was correctly solved.

4.  The formula for finding the intelligence quotient is

    $$\frac{\text{Mental Age}}{\text{Chronological Age}} \times 100$$

    A child who is five chronologically and mentally would have an IQ of 100: 5/5 x 100 = 100.

    Find the following IQs:

    (a) MA 7, CA 5 _____

    (b) MA 4, CA 5 _____

    (c) MA 6, CA 5 _____

5.  The major difference between the Stanford Binet IQ test and the Wechsler Test is that in addition to the _____ part as on the Binet test, the Wechsler test included a nonverbal part, or _____.

---

Name _____ Date _____ Period _____

6.  One important factor which influences intelligence test scores is the _____

    _____, which may differ greatly from culture to culture.

7.  Studies which show the role of heredity on intelligence were done on _____

    _____ (who have the same genetic make-up).

8.  _____ tests are costly and time-consuming, whereas

    _____ tests cost less in time and money.

9.  One major criticism of intelligence tests is the tests are constructed by and contain material

    from the _____.

10. A person who produces original, workable ideas, is said to be _____.

11. A _____ is a tendency to use the same solution over and over. _____

    _____ is finding a different, novel solution to a problem.

12. _____ is defined as below average intellectual functioning

    in which the person is unable to handle tasks appropriate to his or her physical age. There

    are five basic classifications. Explain each, and give the IQ range for each.

    (a) borderline mental retardation _____

    _____

    _____

    (b) mild mental retardation _____

    _____

    _____

    (c) moderate mental retardation _____

    _____

    _____

    (d) severe mental retardation _____

    _____

    _____

(e) profound mental retardation _____

_____

_____

13. What are some methods of treatment for the mentally retarded?

_____

_____

_____

_____

Name _____ Date _____ Period _____

# WORSHEET

**DIRECTIONS:** Write your answer in the space provided.

1. The type of IQ test which saves time and money because it may be given to large groups of people at the same time is the _____.

2. The term for below average intellectual functioning that prevents a person from being able to perform at the level appropriate for his or her age is _____.

3. Binet's definition of intelligence includes _____, _____, _____, and _____.

4. The classes of mental retardation are _____, _____, _____, _____, and _____.

5. Solving problems in the same old way is called _____. Getting out of the traditional mold and finding a novel solution to a problem is _____.

6. The ability to understand and adapt to the environment using a combination of inherited abilities and learning experiences is called _____.

7. The developer of the first IQ test is _____.

8. The revision and perfection of the first IQ test is called _____.

9. A measure of intelligence originally obtained by comparing mental age as determined by testing with chronological age is called _____.

10. Differentiate between intelligence and creativity.

   _____

   _____

   _____

11. Differentiate between verbal scale and performance scale.

   _____

   _____

   _____

# DISCUSSION

1. There is much controversy over whether IQ is influenced more by heredity or environment. Write a short paper which supports the argument for heredity. Now, write another short paper which supports environment. What do YOU think?

2. Which of the two types of intelligence tests discussed in the text, the Stanford-Binet and the Wechsler, seems to be more fair in general than the other? Why?

3. Can a very intelligent person also be creative? Does intelligence also mean creativity? Does creativity always mean that a person is highly intelligent? Explain your reasoning.

4. Cultural differences may greatly influence definitions of intelligence within cultures. Name some differences in some cultures which could greatly influence IQ.

5. Even if intellectual ability is a matter of heredity, environmental factors may still play a vital part in its development. Name and explain some environmental factors which may enhance intelligence, and name some factors in the environment which may retard or hinder intellectual development.

6. Creativity is the result of mental processes which result in original, workable ideas. On a sheet of paper write the word "newspaper." Under this word write as many uses for the newspaper as you can think of, and try to be creative. (Limit yourself to at least 20). Now analyze the list and determine how many of these uses could be considered truly creative. Perhaps the entire class could make such lists and discuss the creativity of the ideas.

# ACTIVITIES

1.  Make an appointment with a guidance counselor or school psychologist and interview him/her about the types of tests used in your school, especially intelligence tests. Make a list of questions you have always wanted answered on the type of tests you take and their uses.

2.  If your school or any local agency has a special education program, find out what criteria are used in determining who will participate in the program. If possible, you may want to investigate any of your state agencies which provide training and/or care for the mentally retarded. What type of training do they receive? How are their needs met? What kind of care do they receive? If there is an institution for the mentally retarded in your area, perhaps your teacher could arrange a field trip to tour the facility.

3.  After you get the information on agencies dealing with the mentally retarded, try to find out if the training equips the mentally retarded individual to work in the community. Try to find out if any businesses in your community employ the mentally retarded, and what kind of jobs they do. If possible, arrange an interview with an employer of the mentally retarded. Write out questions beforehand. These may include such items as "What kind of work do they do?" "How effective are they in performing assigned tasks?" "What is the rate of absenteeism?" "How well do they interact with the other employees?" If possible, present your findings to the class.

4.  What special provisions are made in your school for the gifted students? Are there any community or college agencies near you which make special provisions for these students? If you were classified as a gifted student, what special programs would you like to have added to your school curriculum? What community agencies or projects would you like to see established?

5.  Write your own definition of intelligence. Ask some of your family members, other relatives and a few friends to write their definitions of intelligence. Compare the definitions with the one given in the book. How many of your definitions compare favorably with the text definition? How well did your own definition compare with the definition in the text? Explain.

6.  Identical twins come from the same fertilized egg, therefore they have the same or identical heredity. It has happened that some identical twins were for some reason separated at birth and reared in separate and often very different environments. Studies done on identical twins who did not know they had a twin, and who grew up in different environments, have shown some startling and fascinating results. Do some research on this topic and list all the similarities between the twins that you can find. How do you account for these? What are some major differences? How do you explain these?

7. Fill in the chart below with those things which you would classify as intelligence or creativity. Several examples are listed to get you started. Could some be both intelligence and creativity?

| INTELLIGENCE | CREATIVITY |
| --- | --- |
| Verbal ability<br>Problem solving | Artistic ability<br>Problem solving |

## Chapter 10    Infancy and Childhood

• • • • • • • • • • • • • • • • • • • • • • • • • • • • • • • • • • • •

## VOCABULARY REVIEW

**DIRECTIONS:** Define the following terms:

1. heredity _____

   _____

2. environment _____

   _____

3. nature/nurture controversy _____

   _____

4. monozygotic twins _____

   _____

5. maturation _____

   _____

6. growth cycle _____

   _____

7. imprinting _____

   _____

8. critical period _____

   _____

9. feral children _____

   _____

10. nuclear family _____

    _____

11. extended family _____

    _____

12. chromosomes _____

_____

13. separation anxiety _____

_____

14. cognitive development _____

_____

15. sensorimotor stage _____

_____

16. object permanence _____

_____

17. preoperational stage _____

_____

18. reversibility _____

_____

19. conservation _____

_____

20. concrete operations stage _____

_____

21. formal operations stage _____

_____

22. preconventional level _____

_____

23. conventional level _____

_____

24. postconventional level _____

_____

# REVIEW/TEST PREPARATION

**A. MULTIPLE CHOICE:** Write the letter of the correct answer in the space provided.

_____ 1. One question which has long been of interest to scientists studying animals and people is that of
  a. parents/teenagers.
  b. nature/nurture controversy.
  c. genetics/phonetics.
  d. environment/etiology.

_____ 2. Ducks and some other birds are programmed to accept a mother at a specific time in development. This is
  a. growth development.
  b. critical period.
  c. maturation.
  d. imprinting.

_____ 3. The nuclear family consists of
  a. parents, children, grandparents.
  b. parents, children, aunts, and uncles.
  c. parents and their children.
  d. parents, children, grandparents, aunts, uncles.

_____ 4. The extended family consists of
  a. parents, children, grandparents.
  b. parents, children, aunts, and uncles.
  c. parents and children in the same house.
  d. nuclear family plus other relatives.

_____ 5. The three stages of moral development are
  a. preconventional, conventional, postconventional.
  b. preoperational, operational, postoperational.
  c. preoccupational, conventional, postoccupational.
  d. preoccupied, semi-occupied, postoccupied.

**B. TRUE/FALSE:** Write **T** if the statement is true or **F** if the statement is false.

_____ 1. The studies done on monozygotic twins seem to lend support to the nature side in the nature/nurture question.

_____ 2. Monozygotic twins come from the same fertilized egg and therefore have the same genetic make-up.

_____ 3. Dizygotic twins are always either both males or both females.

_____ 4. Parents may teach a child to walk very early by constant practice.

_____ 5. A child who walks and talks at an age earlier than the norm, or average, age for these processes is usually far above average in intelligence.

_____ 6. Today many families consist of a single parent and a child or children.

_____ 7. In families where both parents work, the most important thing where children are concerned is that they feel loved and cared for.

_____ 8. The role of the father as the sole breadwinner has changed very little in recent times.

_____ 9. Children raised by authoritative parents are usually self-confident.

_____ 10. Language develops in young children differently in different cultures.

**C. COMPLETION:** Write the missing word(s) in the blank.

1. An automatic, orderly, and sequential process of physical and mental development is known as _____.

2. A _____ is when learning a skill or making an association occurs only during a specific time period in an animal's maturation.

3. The word used to describe children supposedly raised by animals is _____, meaning "wild, untamed."

4. Child abuse may be both _____ and _____.

5. From about nine months through about 18 months of age, children suffer from what is called _____.

6. Piaget's four stages of cognitive development are _____, _____, _____, and _____.

7. The _____ means that if a relationship goes in one direction, it can be turned around and go the opposite direction, too.

8. _____ means that you can change some of an object's characteristics while keeping others the same.

9. Influences on the developing child, other than parents, are _____,

   _____, _____, _____, and

   _____.

10. Since sounds, words, word arrangement, and accents all vary from culture to culture, it is

    obvious that the _____ plays a critical role in speech development.

# WORKSHEET

**DIRECTIONS:** Unscramble the words to find answers to the following:

1.  Contrasting views of how we gain certain characteristics

    rauten/runuter                                        _____

2.  Automatic, sequential process of physical and mental development

    ramutation                                            _____

3.  Children supposedly reared by animals

    flare                                                 _____

4.  Parents and children living in the same house

    clearun mailfy                                        _____

5.  The basic unit of heredity

    neges                                                 _____

6.  A skill or association occurs only during a specific time of development

    tircical droipe                                       _____

7.  Nuclear family plus other relatives living in the same house

    dexented filmay                                       _____

8.  The biological process in which the young of certain species follow and become attached to their mothers.

    pintrimgin                                            _____

9.  Characteristics obtained directly from the genes

    dethirey                                              _____

10. The baby's fear of being away from the parent; the desire to avoid strangers

    peartasion xyatnei                                    _____

# DISCUSSION

1. The nature (heredity)/nurture (environment) controversy has raged for years, and still is not settled in that there are those who argue for one side, others for the other side. Write a brief paragraph on the importance of each on the developing child. Be sure to include the studies on monozygotic twins. Then write a paragraph setting forth the one you favor and why.

2. Explain what is meant by "Development within a species is orderly and specific."

3. Why couldn't the child, Genie, discussed in the text move beyond a five-year-old's speech level?

4. There are three basic styles of parenting. Name and explain these three.

5. How may the environment affect the maturation processes (negative and positive effects)?

6. What are the sex differences in growth cycles?

7. Define and explain imprinting. Does this apply to humans? Explain.

8. Explain the critical period in relation to animals and humans.

9. Write a brief paragraph on feral children. Be sure to include your own thoughts on the subject.

10. What is meant by the nuclear family? Extended family? How would you classify your own family? Which would you prefer, and why?

11. The question of the effect on children of having both parents work outside the home is of paramount importance in today's society. What are the pros and cons of this issue? What is your own opinion?

12. For years, fathers were pretty much in the background of family life, seen chiefly as breadwinner and stern disciplinarian. This is not true of the modern father. What are some of the changes the role of father has undergone recently? Do you think the role should be changed even further?

13. What are some important influences on the growing child besides the parents? How may these influences positively or negatively effect the child?

14. Child abuse is another emerging issue of great importance. This means psychological as well as physical abuse. What are some factors which may contribute to both forms of abuse?

15. One of the first anxiety-producing events in a baby's life is called separation anxiety. Explain the significance of this in relation to the child and the parent.

16. Around four years of age children develop perfectly normal fears of monsters and the dark. Do you agree with using a night light to help the child through this trying time? Why or why not?

17. Name and explain Piaget's four stages in cognitive development.

18. In the preoperational stage, two events occur, called reversibility and conservation. Explain both.

19. Kohlberg has developed a system of moral development in which there are three stages. Identify these three stages and give the basis for moral reasoning in each.

20. Trace the process of the development of language and its rules.

# ACTIVITIES

1.  Some manufacturers of toys and other gadgets claim that their products will help increase intellectual development in young children. Visit a toy store and check through some of these toys. Note especially the claims listed on the packaging. If display models are available, use them to see how the toy works. Write a report on several of these toys, stating the purpose of the toy and how it works. Note the ages on the labels, and in light of Piaget's stages of cognitive development, give your opinion on whether or not the toy will be effective.

2.  There is an increasing number of schools which claim to educate two-, three-, and four-year-old children beyond their normal capacities. Do research in news periodicals and newspapers and write a report on this new educational development. An important thing to remember: maturational readiness.

3.  Child abuse is an issue which has come to the attention of the public. Research this topic and write a report on it. Some things to consider: Common characteristics of child abusers; effects of physical abuse on the child; effects of psychological abuse on the child; differences between those who abuse only physically and those who abuse only psychologically; do abusers use a combination of physical and psychological abuse? If there are agencies in your area which deal with this problem, you may wish to interview one of the personnel. You may also obtain much information from this source.

4.  Read the following situation and write the typical responses in the chart below on Kohlberg's stages of moral development:

    Steve is a high school senior who lives with his widowed mother. They have just learned that she is dying of an almost incurable disease. The drug department of a local hospital has the medicine that could save her, but it costs $25,000. Steve and his mother do not have the money to pay for the medicine and they have no way to raise the money. The hospital refused to let them have the drug. One night, in desperation, Steve broke into the drug department and took the amount of the drug his mother needed. Do you think Steve should have done this?

    Typical Preconventional Reasoning
    1.
    2.
    3.
    4.

    Typical Conventional Reasoning
    1.
    2.
    3.

    Typical Postconventional Reasoning
    1.
    2.
    3.

Name _____ Date _____ Period _____

## Chapter 11      *Adolescence*

●●●●●●●●●●●●●●●●●●●●●●●●●●●●●●●●●●●●●●●●●●●●●

---

## VOCABULARY

---

**DIRECTIONS:** Fill in the blank space with the letter of the correct term.

a. adolescence
b. juvenile delinquency
c. anorexia nervosa
d. puberty
e. hormones
f. pituitary gland
g. adrenal glands
h. gonads
i. growth spurt
j. early maturer
k. late maturer
l. eating disorders
m. rite of passage
n. crowds
o. clique

p. gang
q. group identity vs. alienation
r. identity
s. identity confusion
t. fidelity
u. foreclosure
v. negative identity
w. diffusion
x. moratorium
y. identity achievement
z. formal operations
aa. postconventional level
bb. social contracts
cc. universal ethical principles

_____ 1. The period of development between childhood and adulthood

_____ 2. Sex glands

_____ 3. Chemical regulators that control bodily processes such as emotional responses, growth, and sexuality

_____ 4. Groups with fairly loose rules, changeable membership, and usually shared interests

_____ 5. Rebellious, antisocial group with strict rules but not connected with accepted school or social organizations

_____ 6. Developing a sense of one's self as a unique person

_____ 7. Possible results from defining oneself as bad or as a troublemaker

_____ 8. A delay in the commitments normally expected of adults

_____ 9. Stage in which the person has the ability to reason in abstract ways; and use complex thought processes

_____ 10. The term for concepts such as justice and honor

_____ 11. Prepares the body for an emergency; also involved in sexual maturation

_____ 12. The repeated violation of the law by those aged 17 and younger

_____ 13. The socially recognized movement from adolescence into adulthood; requires some ritual

_____ 14. Uncertainty about who you are, or where you are going

_____ 15. State in which an adolescent accepts the identity and values he or she was given in childhood

_____ 16. Term for agreements based on the "best for everyone" concept

_____ 17. Term for the state in which the adolescent has developed well-defined personal values and self-concepts

_____ 18. An eating disorder that involves severe loss of weight through excessive dieting

_____ 19. One who is a year and a half or more ahead of average development

_____ 20. Tightly-knit group with limited membership and strict rules of behavior, with common school-related interests

_____ 21. The state of having no clear idea of one's identity and not attempting to find one

_____ 22. Last stage of moral development in which personal ethics and human rights come into play

_____ 23. Idea that early adolescents either belong to a group or feel lost

_____ 24. Controls growth hormones and activates other glands (master gland of the body)

_____ 25. One who is a year and a half behind average growth

_____ 26. Term for being faithful to one's ideals and values; loyalty

_____ 27. The time of sexual maturation

_____ 28. A rapid increase in growth during puberty

_____ 29. Conditions in which the person cannot read the body's nutritional needs and eats or refuses to eat for the wrong reasons

# REVIEW/TEST PREPARATION

**MULTIPLE CHOICE:** Write the letter of the correct answer in the space provided.

_____ 1. Most teenagers handle puberty much better than some people think. The percentage of those who do have trouble adjusting is
a. 18 percent.
b. 15 percent.
c. 20 percent.
d. 10 percent.

_____ 2. Differences in level of maturation between boys and girls are greatest in
a. early adolescence.
b. middle adolescence.
c. late adolescence.
d. early puberty.

_____ 3. An early maturer is one who is about
a. two and a half years ahead of peers.
b. a year ahead of peers.
c. a year and a half ahead of peers.
d. two years ahead of peers.

_____ 4. A late maturer is one who is about
a. two and a half years behind peers.
b. a year behind peers.
c. a year and a half behind peers.
d. two years behind peers.

_____ 5. Groups which are fairly large, loosely structured, and have fluctuating memberships are called
a. mobs.
b. cliques.
c. gangs.
d. crowds.

_____ 6. Delaying of commitments of adulthood to find one's identity is called
a. identity crisis.
b. moratorium.
c. identity confusion.
d. maturation.

_____ 7. Adolescents who accept the identity and values given in childhood are in a state of
a. moratorium.
b. foreclosure.
c. diffusion.
d. fidelity.

Name _____ Date _____ Period _____

_____ 8. Adolescents who have no clear idea of their identity, and are not trying to find one, are in a state of
   a. moratorium.
   b. foreclosure.
   c. diffusion.
   d. fidelity.

_____ 9. According to Piaget, adolescents are in the
   a. sensorimotor stage.
   b. preoperational stage.
   c. concrete operations stage.
   d. formal operations stage.

_____ 10. According to Kohlberg's stages of moral development, an individual who makes decisions about right and wrong according to basic principles has reached the
   a. preconventional level.
   b. conventional level.
   c. postconventional level.
   d. unconventional level.

**COMPLETION:** Write the missing word(s) in the blank.

1. Adolescence is divided into three phases, _____,
   _____, and _____.

2. _____ is sexual maturation.

3. Hormones control body growth and are responsible for sexual maturation. Three glands which interact during puberty are the _____, _____
   _____, and _____.

4. Rapid periods of growth during adolescence are called _____.

5. Excessive dieting can lead to _____, a condition with severe physical effects.

6. When a change in status is recognized by a formal ceremony, it is called _____
   _____.

7. Small groups made up of adolescents who have common school-related interests are known as _____.

8. Groups of adolescents who have an antisocial attitude and are based on out-of-school interests are _____.

9.  According to Erikson, the period of development during early adolescence is _____

    _____.

10. Developing a sense of one's self as an individual means achieving _____.

    Never attaining this goal results in _____.

11. Being faithful to one's ideals and values, and loyal to those we care about in spite of their

    actions, is called _____.

12. For some adolescents, a _____ results from foreclosure.

13. Adolescents with a well-defined self-concept have reached the state of _____

    _____.

14. According to Piaget, when one reasons in an abstract way, he is in the _____

    _____ stage.

15. The first stage in the postconventional level of moral development emphasizes _____

    _____ and the second emphasizes_____.

16. Repeated violations of the law by those 17 and younger is _____.

Name _____ Date _____ Period _____

# WORKSHEET

**DIRECTIONS:** Adolescence is a time of identity search. Identify the following by circling the word in the word search and writing it in the blank space provided.

1. Age from sixteen to nineteen                                   _____

2. Time of sexual maturation                                      _____

3. Body chemicals that control body growth, physical
   change                                                         _____

4. Sex glands                                                     _____

5. Gland which secretes growth hormone                           _____

6. Period of rapid development                                   _____

7. A change in status recognized by a formal ritual             _____

8. Rebellious, antisocial group                                  _____

9. Sense of self                                                 _____

10. Uncertainty about who one is or where one is going          _____

11. Delay in commitments normally expected of adults            _____

12. Being faithful to one's ideals and values                   _____

13. No clear idea of or attempt to find identity                _____

14. Accepting identity and values given in childhood            _____

| D | L | A | T | E | A | D | O | L | E | S | C | E | N | C | E | N |
|---|---|---|---|---|---|---|---|---|---|---|---|---|---|---|---|---|
| N | A | T | E | A | D | M | U | I | R | O | T | A | R | O | M | Y |
| A | R | F | O | R | E | C | L | O | S | U | R | E | S | U | R | E |
| L | F | O | R | E | I | D | E | L | U | R | U | S | U | R | E | L |
| G | A | N | F | I | D | E | L | T | R | E | P | G | A | N | D | S |
| Y | D | R | I | T | E | O | F | P | A | S | S | A | G | E | R | N |
| R | I | T | D | U | N | A | L | A | S | A | H | P | O | A | R | D |
| A | P | U | E | B | T | O | T | Y | I | D | T | A | N | E | N | Y |
| T | U | I | L | T | I | A | I | R | Y | G | W | E | A | M | C | G |
| I | T | O | I | N | T | E | N | S | E | N | O | H | D | E | N | T |
| U | I | T | T | Y | Y | A | R | Y | U | A | R | L | S | I | O | N |
| T | T | Y | Y | G | L | D | E | N | T | F | G | T | Y | C | R | I |
| I | D | E | N | T | I | T | Y | C | O | N | F | U | S | I | O | N |
| P | U | B | E | R | T | Y | I | D | E | N | C | I | N | F | U | S |
| F | I | D | E | H | O | R | M | O | N | E | S | L | D | I | T | Y |

# DISCUSSION

1. At age 21 a person has all the legal rights of an adult. However, at this age many people are still unmarried, in school, and dependent on their parents for financial support. This situation could give rise to a lot of confusion, frustration, and resentment on the part of the parents and the young adult. Explain this from each side.

2. Humans are the only animals who take care of their young over an extensive period of time. There is no other example of this in the animal kingdom. Your author suggested that the tension between parent and child which arises at puberty may make the later separation easier for both parties. What is your opinion? Are you ready to go out on your own? Why or why not?

3. Discuss the factors associated with juvenile delinquency. Is it a proven fact that an adolescent in whose life the factors are present *will* become a juvenile delinquent? Discuss some of the preventive programs.

4. Difference in rates of maturation in boys and girls is most obvious in early adolescence. This difference creates problems in relating to each other. From your own experiences, discuss this situation.

5. Boys who are early maturers and girls who are late maturers are more self-confident and less self-conscious than they would be if the reverse were true. Why do you think this is true?

6. Discuss adolescence in relation to conformity, groups, crowds, cliques, gangs, and peer pressure.

7. Explain what is meant by Erikson's crisis of adolescence, identity versus identity confusion.

8. If a person does achieve Kohlberg's postconventional level of moral reasoning, he or she generally does so by late adolescence. Those who have reached this level make decisions about right and wrong according to basic principles. Assuming you have reached this level, what would you do in the following situations? Explain your reasoning for each answer.

   (a) You did not study for the test you are to have today. Should you look on the paper of someone sitting near you?

   (b) You know you are late if you are not seated in your desk when the tardy bell rings. The teacher was completing some forms at her desk and did not see you enter the room two minutes late. What do you do?

   (c) You were not involved in, but did witness, an incident clearly in violation of school rules. You have been called to the office to tell what you saw. Do you give an accurate report?

   (d) Assume some of your friends were involved in violation of school rules in c. Do you give an accurate report?

9.  Do you think there is really a "generation gap" in our society? Why or why not?

10. Discuss some of the issues which have the most potential for creating tension between parents and adolescents. Some of these may be music, money, curfews, style of clothes, dating, etc.

11. Good communication skills can go a long way in maintaining harmony between adolescents and their parents. Describe a time when you and your parents came into conflict, and analyze how the rules of good communication could have eased the situation.

12. How much responsibility do you have? How much responsibility do your parents retain? How much would you like to have? Describe some personal examples of responsible, adult-like behavior, as well as examples of child-like behavior. Give examples of both types of behavior in some of your friends.

# ACTIVITIES

1. Much tension and dissension is created between parents and teenagers because of the difference in musical tastes. Listen carefully to several of your favorite pieces of music, and write down how the words of the songs have influenced your morals, values, beliefs, and goals. (Be honest!) If the teacher allows, your classmates could do the same, and then have a class discussion/debate on the influence of modern music on teenagers.

2. Answer the following letters to Dear Abbie:

   (a) Dear Abbie,

   My mother wants to know every little thing I do, where I go, who I go with, what I did. She is always asking me how things went in school. This is driving me bananas! What can I do about this?

   Signed,
   Daughter of Nosey

   (b) Dear Abbie,

   I am a 17-year-old high school senior. I have an 11-year-old sister who loves to go in my room and meddle in all my private things. My mother refuses to make her stop. Tell me what to do before I do her bodily harm.

   Signed,
   Frantic

   (c) Dear Abbie,

   My boyfriend lives in another state, and we write to each other three or four times a week. I keep his letters in a special box. Lately I have discovered that my mother has been reading the letters. Abbie, we never say things that are dark secrets or shameful, but they are private. Should I confront my mother with this, or should I find another hiding place for my letters?

   Signed,
   Unsure

3. Every generation of teenagers has its own language, or jargon. Write down the words you and your friends use that are peculiar to your age group, and their meanings. Ask your parents or an adult of about their age to tell you the words they used when they were adolescents, and their meanings, and write these down. Make a comparison between the two. What are the similarities? What are the differences?

4. Adolescence is generally a time when we have a more negative concept of ourselves than we will have at a later time (a few years), yet we all have good qualities which we let become obscured by negative thinking. Complete the 20 "I am. . ." statements with ONLY positive things about yourself. This should make you feel better about yourself.

1. I am _____ .

2. I am _____ .

3. I am _____ .

4. I am _____ .

5. I am _____ .

6. I am _____ .

7. I am _____ .

8. I am _____ .

9. I am _____ .

10. I am _____ .

11. I am _____ .

12. I am _____ .

13. I am _____ .

14. I am _____ .

15. I am _____ .

16. I am _____ .

17. I am _____ .

18. I am _____ .

19. I am _____ .

20. I am _____ .

# Chapter 12     *Adulthood and Aging*

## VOCABULARY

**DIRECTIONS:** Use the clues to complete the crossword puzzle below.

**ACROSS**

1. Period of life when children are grown and move away from home which may cause feelings of uselessness and depression
6. The first stage in the series of stages on approaching death
9. Blockage of blood vessels to the brain causes cerebral
10. Loss of mental faculties in old age

**DOWN**

2. Study of death and methods for coping with it
3. "Change of life period" for women
4. Branch of psychology that studies the aging process and problems of older people
5. A disease involving the loss of chemical nerve cell transmitters and other damage to nerve transmission which result in mental deterioration
7. Care of terminally ill people that emphasizes pain management, comfort, and quality of life
8. Age 40 signals the true beginning of _____

# REVIEW/TEST PREPARATION

**COMPLETION:** Write the missing word(s) in the blank.

1.  Sometime during their 20s and 30s many people begin the adult responsibilities of

    _____, _____ and _____.

2.  Adulthood may be divided into three different periods. The ages 20-39 are called _____

    _____, ages 40-59 are called _____,

    and from 60 on, _____.

3.  One critical ingredient which can contribute to a successful marriage is _____

    _____.

4.  In this country, the age of 40 signals the true beginning of _____.

5.  For some people, _____ is a time for reassessing goals and refocusing

    energies on new things. For others, it is a time of terrible upheaval and loss of purpose.

6.  Some have called the second half of middle adulthood the _____, the

    prime of life.

7.  In general, during middle adulthood, 40-59, men begin to appreciate their more

    _____ characteristics, and women their more _____ ones.

8.  The _____ is the time of life after the children leave home.

9.  At some time in the late 40s to early 50s women go through a change of life called

    _____.

10. People tend to become more satisfied with life in _____.

11. The branch of psychology which is the study of older people is called _____.

12. Indications are that the problems and ailments of old age occur because of _____

    _____.

13. A term often erroneously used to describe many elderly is _____, which means

    deterioration of mental processes.

14. Blockage of blood vessels to the brain, or _____

    may happen in the older person.

15. The major cause of senility is _____, a chemical malfunction

    in the brain.

16. Three basic fears of the elderly are _____, _____,

    and having _____.

17. Two other fears which older people have are _____ and _____.

18. _____ is the study of death and dying.

19. Terminally ill people have three basic fears:

    (a) _____

    (b) _____

    (c) _____

20. According to Elizabeth Kübler-Ross, terminally ill people go through five stages of death:

    _____, _____, _____,

    _____, and _____.

21. _____ focuses on managing pain, promoting comfort, and

    improving the quality of life for people who are terminally ill.

# WORKSHEET

1.  On the chart below fill in the positive and negative aspects of each of the stages.

| STAGES OF ADULTHOOD | |
|---|---|
| Positive | Negative |
| Early adulthood: (20-39) | |
| | |
| Middle Adulthood: (40-59) | |
| | |
| Late Adulthood: (Begins at 60) | |
| | |

Name _____ Date _____ Period _____

2. According to Elizabeth Kübler-Ross, a terminally ill person goes through five stages approaching death. Characterize each.

    (a) Denial _____

    _____

    (b) Anger _____

    _____

    (c) Bargaining _____

    _____

    (d) Depression _____

    _____

    (e) Acceptance _____

    _____

# DISCUSSION

1. The United States has become a divorce-riddled society in which young children are most often the real victims. Discuss the financial and psychological effects of divorce on children.

2. Discuss the female and male roles in modern marriages. Have we made much change? State your opinion.

3. Write about the positive and the negative reactions of people during the mid-life transition.

4. Middle adulthood (40-59) appears to bring some role changes for men and women. Discuss these changes in detail.

5. Much ado has been made about what is known as the empty-nest syndrome, and perhaps for some women it is a traumatic time. Do you think your mother will go through this adjustment with negative results? Do you know women who have suffered from this experience? Explain.

6. Explain what is meant by the "mellow fifties."

7. Explain gerontology, and tell why it is becoming more necessary.

8. Our culture is a youth-worshipping culture, yet aging is an inevitable process. Discuss this aging process. What are some of the concerns of the aging?

9. Our mental processes do change as we grow older. Discuss these changes and any possible causes.

10. We have some erroneous ideas about the intelligence of older people. What are some of the reasons for this? What are some problems concerning older people and intelligence testing?

11. If you are like most of us, you have at some time referred to an older person as senile. What is senility? What percentage of the elderly are actually senile?

12. Discuss the needs and fears of the aged.

13. Many people view retirement as the end of life. Discuss the possible effects of retirement on men and on women. When do you think people should begin planning for retirement? Do you think there should be mandatory retirement? At what age? Why or why not?

14. One big fear of the aged is bereavement. Discuss the effects of the loss of a spouse on the aged survivor.

15. As a culture which places so much emphasis on youth, we tend to view old age as something undesirable. How does this attitude affect the aged? How do they view themselves? How do you view the aged and the aging process?

16. If you were an old person would you want to be in a nursing home? Under what conditions do you think this should be an alternative? What are some possible negative effects on the aged person in such an institution?

17. Do you think there should be a law requiring elderly people to take a driver's test every year before their driver's license could be renewed? Why or why not? At what age do you think this should begin?

18. Death is a part of life. None of us like to think about losing loved ones, and certainly we do not want to think about our own deaths. Carefully consider: What is your attitude toward death? What are the three basic fears of people who are terminally ill?

19. Elizabeth Kübler-Ross says that people who are terminally ill go through five stages. Discuss each of these. Do you think the relatives and good friends of the ill person may go through a similar process? What are some criticisms of the stages of dying?

20. What is thanatology? Discuss some of the current issues regarding death.

# ACTIVITIES

1.  This activity will require that you use your imagination. Below is a chart on which has been listed the life stages in adulthood. Since you are on the threshold of adulthood, imagine that "You Are There" at the various stages and fill in what you think you will be doing, and check whether it is a positive or a negative aspect of each age. Projecting yourself into the future is almost impossible, but use your imagination and be as realistic as you can.

| YOUR ARE THERE | | | |
|---|---|---|---|
| Age | What will you do? | Pos. | Neg. |
| 20–39 | | | |
| 40–59 | | | |
| 60 onward | | | |

2. Visit a nursing home. Arrange beforehand to interview someone in the office. Some questions you may want to ask are: What is the nature of the problem that made it necessary for the person to enter the facility? What percent of the residents are complete invalids (confined to bed)? What percent are able to get around in a wheel chair? What percent are ambulatory? How many have Alzheimer's disease? What kinds of care/therapy are provided? What percent of the residents have family members visit them on a regular basis? Check into the cost of care in the nursing home. This should be an eye-opening experience for you.

3. In addition to providing a place for terminally ill people to live out their lives in comfort away from hospitals, a hospice also has volunteers go to homes of the terminally ill and counsel them and the family members on death and dying. They will do housecleaning and shopping, if necessary. Call a local hospice chapter and arrange an interview. Make your questions beforehand, based on the information given here, and learn as much as you can about this organization.

4. Thanatology is the study of death and methods for coping with it. The word thanatology comes from the Greek word "thanatos," meaning death. Read the poem ''Thanatopsis'' by William Cullen Bryant. He wrote the poem when he was about seventeen or eighteen years old—about your age—and the close of it was written when he was about 27. Write an analysis of the poem. What is the poet's view on death? Reread the last nine lines. What is his poetic advice about how to live? Compare your own thoughts with those of the poet.

5. Make a list of questions you think appropriate to ask a person in each of the stages of adulthood, then interview someone you know - a relative or friend of each age. Write your questions from the information found in this chapter. Be tactful in your wording. After you have compiled your research, compare your findings with what the text says. How close are your findings? What, if any, are differences in the two?

6. A question often asked of young children is, "What do you want to be when you grow up?" You are now in high school, and some of you are pretty sure about your careers or vocations, some still undecided. Write down a life plan for yourself for the next ten years. What do you hope to accomplish in this time period? What are your plans when you graduate from high school—college or entry into the work world? What are your plans for growth and development in your chosen field? Will you marry? Do you plan to have children? Should both partners in the marriage work, even if you have children?

# Chapter 13 — Gender Differences

## VOCABULARY

**DIRECTIONS:** Fill in the blanks with the correct term.

**What Am I?**

| | |
|---|---|
| gender | menstrual cycle |
| hormone | premenstrual syndrome |
| androgen | gender role behavior |
| estrogen | identification |
| spatial skills | androgyny |

1. I am the process of modeling behavior patterns after a member of the same sex. What am I?

   _____

2. I am the male hormone. What am I?

   _____

3. I am anxiety, irritability, and mental confusion resulting from monthly female hormonal changes. What am I?

   _____

4. I am the sex of the individual, male or female. What am I?

   _____

5. I am acts that reflect society's view of what is appropriate for males, and what is appropriate for females. What am I?

   _____

6. I am the quality of having both masculine and feminine characteristics. What am I?

   _____

7. I am the regulators that control bodily processes such as emotional responses, growth, and sexuality. What am I?

   _____

8. I am the monthly event in which the lining of the female uterus is eliminated when the egg has not been fertilized. What am I?

   _____

9. I am the female hormone. What am I?

   _____

10. I am the skill involving the ability to imagine how an object would look if it were moved about in space. What am I?

    _____

# REVIEW/TEST PREPARATION

**MULTIPLE CHOICE:** Write the letter of the correct answer in the space provided.

_____ 1. The two types of hormones we have are
   a. estrogen and progesterone.
   b. androgen and progesterone.
   c. androgen and estrogen.
   d. estrogen and androgyny.

_____ 2. Androgen injected into a human adult female causes increased
   a. passivity.
   b. aggressiveness.
   c. anxiety.
   d. playfulness.

_____ 3. One major biological male/female difference is that the
   a. male works outside the home.
   b. female cries more easily.
   c. male does not show emotion.
   d. female bears the offspring.

_____ 4. Which of the following is true concerning gender differences?
   a. Males are always bigger than females
   b. The sexes are more alike than different
   c. Females are rarely as aggressive as males
   d. There are few similarities between the sexes

_____ 5. Which of the following is true of gender differences in activity level?
   a. Males are more active.
   b. Females are more active.
   c. Males and females are equally active.
   d. Females are easily dominated.

_____ 6. Despite differences in development of skills, overall intellectual ability in both sexes is
   a. very close.
   b. drastically different, male superior.
   c. drastically different, female superior.
   d. identical in every way.

_____ 7. Spatial skills refers to the ability to
   a. put things in the right spaces.
   b. visualize the stars in space.
   c. be alone in open spaces.
   d. imagine how something would look in space.

_____ 8. Which of the following is NOT a reason that studies on gender differences in mathematical ability are inconclusive?
   a. Our society has a bias against females being involved in math.
   b. Teachers and parents expect males to do better than females in math.
   c. Results from studies about gender differences in mathematical ability are consistent.
   d. More males than females claim to "enjoy" math.

_____ 9. Studies on difference in feelings of self-confidence by males and females show
   a. no difference between the sexes.
   b. females feel less self-confidence.
   c. males feel less self-confidence.
   d. great differences between the sexes.

_____ 10. In the drive for success,
   a. males and females are very different.
   b. males are more achievement-oriented.
   c. females are more achievement-oriented.
   d. males and females are about the same.

_____ 11. The myth of great differences between males and females, with males being superior, is generally a result of
   a. social factors.
   b. personal factors.
   c. biological factors.
   d. psychological factors.

_____ 12. In communication, which gender talks more and touches the one to whom he/she is talking?
   a. male
   b. female
   c. This happens about equally for both sexes.
   d. Neither gender touches people they are talking to.

_____ 13. Hormones have an effect on all human beings. Which of the following is true?
   a. Both males and females experience a monthly cycle.
   b. Only the female is subject to a monthly cycle.
   c. Males have no hormones which may alter their behavior.
   d. Females always have a radical reaction during their monthly cycle.

_____ 14. An example of gender role behavior which reflects the societal view of what is appropriate for males versus females is
   a. girls and boys playing with unisex toys.
   b. girls playing with girl dolls, boys with boy dolls.
   c. girls and boys playing with a football.
   d. girls playing with dolls, boys playing with a football.

_____ 15. Boys up to age five whose fathers were not present during this time tend to be
      a. more aggressive.
      b. less aggressive.
      c. very feminine.
      d. "macho."

_____ 16. In families where either the mother or father is usually dominant, the children tend to identify with
      a. the less dominant parent.
      b. the dominant parent.
      c. some other family member.
      d. the father, regardless of whether he is the dominant parent or not.

_____ 17. The term androgyny means
      a. excessive female characteristics.
      b. excessive male characteristics.
      c. having both male and female characteristics.
      d. having neither male or female characteristics.

_____ 18. People who have both masculine and feminine characteristics are
      a. psychologically healthier than those with strong gender identities.
      b. more confused than those with strong gender identities.
      c. socially awkward.
      d. in need of counseling.

_____ 19. A male who sticks only to the traditional male role is
      a. androgynous.
      b. severely limiting his life experiences.
      c. very insecure.
      d. severely restricting his life expectancy.

_____ 20. A female who sticks only to the traditional female role is
      a. severely limiting her life experiences.
      b. leading an unconventional life.
      c. exploring her "masculine" qualities.
      d. the most psychologically healthy type of female.

# WORKSHEET

**COMPLETION:** Write the missing word(s) in the blank.

1. _____ are regulators that control bodily processes such as emotional responses, growth, and sexuality.

2. Two sex hormones are _____, the male hormone, and _____, the female hormone.

3. The only activities that clearly and absolutely belong to one sex are those involved in _____.

4. Gender differences in _____ appear as early as 45 hours.

5. _____ refers to the ability to imagine how something would look in space.

6. Of the two sexes, _____ have greater physical endurance.

7. Research indicates that males and females have a(n) _____ amount of self-confidence.

8. Research indicates that males and females have a(n) _____ drive for success.

9. Because a lot of women are entering the work force, one area of concern has been _____.

10. _____ causes anxiety, irritability, and mental confusion in a small percentage of women.

11. _____ involves acts that reflect society's view of what is appropriate for male versus female.

12. Psychologist Sandra Bem developed the concept of _____, which means that a person has both masculine and feminine characteristics.

# DISCUSSION

1.  The text gives some interesting information on the roles of males and females. Do your ideas and opinions of these roles conflict or coincide with what the text says? In what way do they differ? How are they alike? After reading the material, have your ideas changed any? If so, how?

2.  Discuss the ways altering hormones may affect one's behavior.

3.  The author says that the major difference between males and females is in the reproductive process. Many people have thought that there were other major differences. Discuss these differences and relate what the author says to your discussion.

4.  One major influence in determining sex role behavior is environmental influences. How has this been such a major factor?

5.  Discuss the following in relation to males and females: self-confidence, drive for success, maternal drive, and hormonal cycles.

6.  For decades, psychologists have been studying characteristics which people want and value in future spouses. Discuss these in terms of female preferences and male preferences. Why are these differences so far-reaching? Male status? Female status?

7.  Much gender role behavior is a result of societal expectations. Fully explain this. What are some expectations and their results? Do you agree with these expectations? Why or why not?

8.  A most interesting part of this chapter is "Mixing Gender Roles." Fully discuss this, including the concept androgyny. What is your opinion of this concept?

9.  We live in an ever-changing world, including changes in male and female roles. Discuss the traditional roles for men and women and contrast them with the modern trend of more blending the two. In view of more women participating in the work world, what do you think of the emerging changes?

# ACTIVITIES

1.  Below is a chart containing a list of occupations. Beside each is a place for you to check whether the occupation is considered strictly masculine or strictly feminine, or both. Following this is an identical chart which you are to ask a parent or someone in the parent's age group (should be in their 50s), to check in accordance with the idea of masculine/feminine occupations when they were your age. Compare the two charts and note any differences. Then answer the questions which follow the charts.

| OCCUPATION | Masculine | Feminine | Both |
|---|---|---|---|
| 1. Architect | | | |
| 2. Teacher | | | |
| 3. Plumber | | | |
| 4. Doctor | | | |
| 5. Electrician | | | |
| 6. Sales Clerk | | | |
| 7. Secretary | | | |
| 8. Lawyer | | | |
| 9. Bookkeeper | | | |
| 10. Truck Driver | | | |
| 11. Nurse | | | |
| 12. Engineer | | | |
| 13. Interior Decorator | | | |
| 14. Hair Dresser | | | |
| 15. Bus Driver | | | |
| 16. Mechanic | | | |
| 17. Construction Worker | | | |
| 18. Postal Delivery Person | | | |
| 19. Bricklayer | | | |
| 20. Pharmacist | | | |

Name _____ Date _____ Period _____

| OCCUPATION | Masculine | Feminine | Both |
|---|---|---|---|
| 1. Architect | | | |
| 2. Teacher | | | |
| 3. Plumber | | | |
| 4. Doctor | | | |
| 5. Electrician | | | |
| 6. Sales Clerk | | | |
| 7. Secretary | | | |
| 8. Lawyer | | | |
| 9. Bookkeeper | | | |
| 10. Truck Driver | | | |
| 11. Nurse | | | |
| 12. Engineer | | | |
| 13. Interior Decorator | | | |
| 14. Hair Dresser | | | |
| 15. Bus Driver | | | |
| 16. Mechanic | | | |
| 17. Construction Worker | | | |
| 18. Postal Delivery Person | | | |
| 19. Bricklayer | | | |
| 20. Pharmacist | | | |

After comparing the two charts, answer the following questions.

(a) Has there been a significant change in attitudes concerning gender roles and employment since your parent or other adult was your age? If so, what?

_____

_____

(b) Would you want your spouse to be employed in a position which was considered strictly for the sex opposite of your spouse's sex? Why or why not?

_____

_____

(c)  Which occupations showed the greatest change between your chart and that of the other person?

_____

_____

_____

(d)  How do you account for the differences, if any, between the two charts?

_____

_____

_____

2.  This would be a good exercise for the entire class. After completing the following sentences, students could take turns reading them aloud and discussing attitudes and beliefs about each one. If this is not possible, perhaps you could get a small group of friends to participate in the exercise.

Complete the following:

What I like most about women is...
What I like most about men is...
One thing I dislike about women is...
One thing I dislike about men is...
An effeminate-acting man is...
A masculine-acting woman is...
A woman who is self-sufficient and independent is...
A man who shows his emotions is...
Paying women less than men for the same job is...
A woman who is success oriented is...
A man who is success oriented is...
A woman who shows her emotions is...

3.  Read several fairy tales and nursery rhymes. How are the males presented? How are the females presented? Is there a significant difference in how males and females are presented in these fairy tales as compared to how they are presented on television shows? In soap operas? Consider some modern songs. How are females depicted? How are males depicted? Is there a reflection of change of attitude toward role expectations for men and women?

4.  Now that you are almost through the adolescent stage of your life, make up a list of dos and don'ts which you would like to have had as you began this turbulent and exciting period in your development.

# Chapter 14    Theories of Personality

## VOCABULARY

**A. DIRECTIONS:** Fill in the blank space with the letter of the correct term.

a. personality
b. psychoanalytic theory
c. unconscious
d. free association
e. repression
f. libido
g. id
h. ego
i. superego
j. collective unconscious

k. persona
l. Neo-Freudians
m. behaviorism
n. reinforcements
o. modeling
p. ideal self
q. fully functioning individual
r. self-actualized
s. personality traits
t. archetypes

_____ 1. Freudian term for internal energy forces that continuously seek discharge

_____ 2. The more or less permanent personality characteristics that a person has

_____ 3. Freudian process in which a person says everything that appears in his or her mind, even if the ideas or images seem unconnected

_____ 4. A personality theory that focuses on overt acts or behaviors

_____ 5. Events that follow responses and strengthen the tendency to repeat those responses

_____ 6. Jung's term for the portion of a person that contains ideas or archetypes shared by the whole human race

_____ 7. Rogers's term for someone who has become what he or she should be

_____ 8. Freudian psychological unit roughly synonymous with the conscience

_____ 9. A person's broad, long-lasting patterns of behavior

_____ 10. Those psychoanalysts who broke away from Freud to emphasize social forces in the unconscious

_____ 11. Freudian psychological unit containing basic needs and drives

_____ 12. Maslow's term for the state of having brought to life the full potential of our skills

_____ 13. Jung's term for inherited universal concepts

_____ 14. Bandura's term for learning by imitating others

_____ 15. Freudian psychological unit that is based in reality; the "self" that allows controlled id expression within the boundaries set by the superego

_____ 16. Rogers's term for the goal of each person's development; the self each person would like to be

_____ 17. A theory that personality is based on impulses and needs in the unconscious

_____ 18. Jung's term for a "mask" people wear to hide what they really are or feel

_____ 19. The process of pushing the needs and desires that cause guilt into the unconscious

_____ 20. According to psychoanalytic belief, the part of the mind that is beyond consciousness. Although we are unaware of its contents, they strongly affect our behavior.

**B. DIRECTIONS:** Define the following terms:

1. cardinal traits _____

   _____

2. central traits _____

   _____

3. secondary traits _____

   _____

4. surface traits _____

   _____

5. source traits _____

   _____

6. extraversion _____

   _____

7. emotional stability _____

   _____

Name _____ Date _____ Period _____

## REVIEW/TEST PREPARATION

**COMPLETION:** Write the missing word(s) in the blank.

1. A theory that personality is based on impulses and needs in the unconscious is known as

   _____.

2. _____ is the founder of psychoanalysis.

3. The physical symptom that comes from a psychological problem is _____.

4. The part of our mind that is beyond consciousness is the _____.

5. Freudian process which a person says everything that appears in his or her mind even if the

   ideas seem unconnected is _____.

6. When needs and desires that cause guilt are pushed into the unconscious, it is called

   _____.

7. Freudian term for internal energy forces that continually seek discharge, called the

   _____.

8. According to Freud, the mind is divided into three parts: the _____ which is the part

   containing basic needs and drives; the _____ which is synonymous with

   the conscience; and the _____, the self concerned with reality, and acts as mediator

   between the other two.

9. In the _____ of development, feeding and weaning are the child's

   main issue

10. In the _____, the child's major concern is toilet training.

11. The _____ is the stage during which the child experiences

    romantic interest in the apposite sex parent, and hostility toward the same sex parent.

12. During the _____, the child's earlier conflicts are hidden.

13. The stage when people seek an appropriate marital partner and earlier conflicts reappear

    _____.

14. _____ was a Swiss psychoanalyst who broke with Freud and

    advanced the concept of the _____.

15. Jung's term for a "mask" people wear to hide what they really are or feel is _____.

16. Psychoanalysts who broke with Freud to emphasize social forces in the unconscious are

    known as _____.

17. One who broke with Freud and focused on the human need for love was _____.

18. Another who broke with Freud and emphasized the concept of inferiority was _____

    _____.

19. The theorist who divided life into eight stages is _____.

20. A theory which focuses on overt acts or behaviors is called _____.

21. The best known of the behaviorists is _____.

22. _____ are events that follow responses and strengthen the

    tendency to repeat those responses.

23. Albert Bandura is the behaviorist who developed the concept of _____.

24. The _____ psychologists emphasized the whole person and

    accepted the person as an individual human with good qualities.

25. Carl Rogers sees our biggest problem as living up to what he calls our _____.

26. When we have become what we should be, we have become a _____

    _____.

27. Abraham Maslow developed the idea that when one has brought to life the full potential of

    his or skills, he or she is _____.

28. More or less permanent personality characteristics are called _____

    _____.

29. Recent studies suggest that there are three traits that tended to remain the same regardless
    of age. These are

    (a) _____

    (b) _____

    (c) _____

30. Recent studies suggest that five personality factors seem in large part to be inherited or at least appear at an early age. These are

(a) _____

(b) _____

(c) _____

(d) _____

(e) _____

# WORKSHEET

**DIRECTIONS:** Circle the names of the personality theorists, then fill in the blanks below with the correct name.

```
S  K  I  N  H  E  R  S  R
M  A  R  A  O  W  S  K  I
E  R  I  K  R  N  E  I  E
B  U  N  D  N  J  A  N  R
A  D  F  R  E  U  D  N  I
D  N  U  R  Y  N  L  E  K
B  A  N  R  O  G  E  R  S
M  B  A  N  M  A  R  L  O
H  W  O  L  S  A  M  Y  N
```

_____  1. Father of psychoanalysis

_____  2. Defines personality strictly in terms of behavior

_____  3. Introduced concept of collective unconscious

_____  4. Claimed humans are most anxious about not getting enough love

_____  5. People spend lives trying to avoid feelings of inferiority

_____  6. Divided life into eight stages

_____  7. Says much of our personality comes from modeling our behavior after others

_____  8. Believes that humans are basically good

_____  9. Says the person strives to become a self-actualized individual

# DISCUSSION

1. Four major theories of personality which are covered in this chapter are psychoanalysis, social psychoanalysis, behaviorism, and humanism. Compare and contrast these four on how they view the individual, the unconscious, the environment, behavior, and the self.

2. A brief sketch of the life of the major theorists is given. Explain how the events in the life of each of these may have influenced the development of his theory.

3. The view of personality is different for each of these theorists. Freud claimed that one's personality is pretty well set by the age of five years. How do the other theorists view personality?

4. Freud used the free association technique to reach material in the unconscious. Explain how this works.

5. Repression is the process of pushing painful or undesirable material out of conscious awareness. Yet the material is still there and active. Explain.

6. Explain how the id, the ego, and the superego interact.

7. What are some major contributions by Freud to the field of psychology?

8. Jung introduced the concept of collective unconscious. Explain this term and relate how he believed it influenced personality.

9. Explain how Horney's ideas about the human need for love may affect the developing personality.

10. Adler says that people spend their lives trying to dominate and control others to avoid feeling inferior. What is meant by this?

11. Erikson's theory of personality development says that we may change at any time during the various stages of our lives. Discuss these eight stages and the changes one may make going through them.

12. Explain the behavioral approach to personality development.

13. Bandura modified or changed his approach to behaviorism. Explain.

14. Rogers believes that people are basically good. How is his approach to personality different from the ones already discussed?

15. What does Maslow mean by the self-actualized person?

16. Two recent studies suggest that we seem to have inherited, or acquired at an early age, three traits which tend to remain the same regardless of age. Compare these two studies. Do you agree? Why or why not?

## ACTIVITIES

1.  Freud's theory describes five stages in the development of personality. The developing person faces conflicts in each of the stages which must be successfully resolved in order to become a healthy personality. Fill in beside each stage in the chart the task confronting the individual, and the consequences if it is improperly handled.

| FREUD: STAGES OF PERSONALITY DEVELOPMENT | | |
| --- | --- | --- |
| | Task | Possible Problems |
| Oral Stage | | |
| Anal Stage | | |
| Phallic Stage | | |
| Latency Stage | | |
| Genital Stage | | |

2.  Write an autobiography. Keeping in mind what the personality theorists in this chapter have said, write about significant events in your life and how you think they have influenced your personality. What part do you believe environment played? How much of what you are do you attribute to heredity? What are those things about you that make you uniquely you?

3.  Write a paragraph about your ideal self, how you would really like to be. Even though this is an "ideal" self, try to be realistic. Now write a paragraph about your real self. Compare the two. How near do you think you are to becoming the ideal self? If you were realistic in your writing, the ideal self should give you a goal to strive for. Note behaviors you may change in striving for your ideal self and work on these.

# Chapter 15

## *Measuring Personality and Personal Abilities*

## VOCABULARY

**DIRECTIONS:** Fill in the blanks with the correct term.

| | |
|---|---|
| psychological test | Scholastic Assessment Test |
| standardization | achievement test |
| norms | vocational interest test |
| validity | Strong-Campbell Interest test |
| reliability | halo effect |
| personality inventory | reverse halo |
| projective test | standoutishness |
| Rorschach test | situational assessment |
| Thematic Apperception Test | MMPI-2 |
| aptitude test | California Psychological Inventory |
| aptitude | |

1.  The situation in which a person with one negative characteristic is assumed to have other negative traits

    _____

2.  Personality inventory most often used in schools

    _____

3.  Test measuring inner feelings elicited by a vague stimulus such as an ink blot or an unclear picture

    _____

4.  The process of looking at how the circumstances surrounding an event influence people responding to that event

    _____

5.  The most widely used personality inventory

    _____

6.  Pattern of test answers from different types of people

    _____

7. Measure of a test's consistency

_____

8. Objective measure of what people know, how they act, think, and feel, and what their goals are

_____

9. Tests that measure one's special skills (carpentry, medicine, etc.)

_____

10. Most widely used vocational interest test based on answers of people successful in certain fields

_____

11. Tests that measure the amount of specific material remembered from the classroom

_____

12. A list of items about a person's beliefs, habits, hopes, needs, and desires

_____

13. The extent to which a test measures what it is supposed to measure

_____

14. The situation in which a person who has one positive characteristic is assumed to have other positive traits

_____

15. Doing or wearing something that is so startling it distracts observers from noticing one's real abilities

_____

16. An ink blot projective test

_____

17. One's special skills, such as carpentry or medicine as measured by an aptitude test

_____

18. A test that attempts to predict what occupational area an individual will like

   _____

19. The process of developing clear directions for taking, scoring, and interpreting a test

   _____

20. A projective test using unclear pictures about which people make up stories

   _____

21. Test designed to measure ability to do college work

   _____

# REVIEW/TEST PREPARATION

**MULTIPLE CHOICE:** Write the letter of the correct answer in the space provided.

_____ 1. Psychological tests are used to try to
   a. discover hidden secrets and motives.
   b. separate criminals from non-criminals.
   c. determine failures from successes.
   d. find out what a person is really like.

_____ 2. Trying to find out what is normal, expected responses for most people in a specific group is called
   a. setting a precedent.
   b. establishing norms.
   c. establishing consistency.
   d. setting up guidelines.

_____ 3. If a test is valid, it measures
   a. how truthful one is.
   b. the effect of intelligence.
   c. what it is supposed to.
   d. success or failure rates.

_____ 4. Reliability means the answers must be
   a. fairly accurate.
   b. reasonably consistent over time.
   c. more right than wrong.
   d. complete.

_____ 5. A personality inventory is a test about
   a. one's beliefs, habits, hopes, needs, and desires.
   b. one's lack of personality.
   c. how much personality is still needed.
   d. how personalities may clash.

_____ 6. In projective tests, the test-taker projects
   a. his or her feelings onto the test administrator.
   b. his or her attitudes onto paper.
   c. the innermost self onto the stimulus provided.
   d. his or her future plans onto paper.

_____ 7. The Rorschach Ink Blot Test is a(an)
   a. personality inventory.
   b. projective test.
   c. attitude adjustment test.
   d. intelligence test.

_____ 8. Aptitude tests are designed to measure one's
   a. capacity for hard work.
   b. academic ability.
   c. skills and abilities in certain fields.
   d. intellectual capacity.

_____ 9. Achievement tests are designed to measure
   a. what you remember from the classroom.
   b. occupational aptitude.
   c. creativity.
   d. intelligence.

_____ 10. A test designed to predict college work is the
   a. Mathematic Aptitude Test.
   b. Verbal Skills Test.
   c. Scholastic Assessment Test.
   d. Rorschach Ink Blot Test.

_____ 11. One of the most used tests to discover a student's interests is
   a. Stanford-Binet IQ Test.
   b. Rorschach Ink Blot Test.
   c. Scholastic Assessment Test.
   d. Strong-Campbell Interest Inventory.

_____ 12. When a person comes off well in an interview because he or she shows one positive trait and is thus believed to have many positive traits, this is called
   a. the halo effect.
   b. the reverse halo effect.
   c. standoutishness.
   d. the norm effect.

_____ 13. When one negative trait gives the impression of having many negative traits, this is called
   a. the halo effect.
   b. the reverse halo effect.
   c. standoutishness.
   d. the norm effect.

_____ 14. This may occur when one is dressed in a somewhat flashy manner for an interview.
   a. the halo effect
   b. the reverse halo effect
   c. standoutishness
   d. the norm effect

_____ 15. Researchers engaged in situational assessment evaluate performance
   a. in various situations.
   b. in unique job situations.
   c. compared with co-workers.
   d. under pressure.

_____ 16. The most widely used personality inventory is
   a. MMPI-2.
   b. Rorschach.
   c. Scholastic Assessment Test.
   d. California Psychological Inventory.

# WORKSHEET

**DIRECTIONS:** Write the missing word(s) in the blank.

1.  Sally is a high school senior contemplating attending college. What test must she take?

    _____

2.  Roger left his part time job early to interview for a position in an office. He had on work clothes which he wore to work in the warehouse of a local plumbing supply company. What effect might this create?

    _____

3.  Jane wore her nice gray suit, a white blouse, and shoes with medium high heels to interview for a secretarial position. What effect will she create on the interviewer?

    _____

4.  Jim wore a pink and white checked sport coat, white pants, a hot pink shirt, and bright yellow bow tie for his interview for a new job. What effect did he create?

    _____

5.  When we want to know the normal, expected responses for most people in a specific group, what is being done?

    _____

6.  If a test measures what it is supposed to, we say it is

    _____ .

7.  When answers to tests are reasonably consistent over time, this means the test is

    _____ .

8.  When we wish to learn something about a person's beliefs, habits, hopes, needs, and desires, we would use what kind of test?

    _____

9.  When the test-taker is shown a series of pictures, drawings, or inkblots and told to tell what he sees, what do we call these tests?

    _____

10. What is the most famous projective test?

   _____

11. When a person has a special ability or skill, like for carpentry or medicine, what is this called?

   _____

12. What are tests which measure what has been learned?

   _____

13. Tests which help a person pinpoint a certain area of work in which he has a special interest are called

   _____ .

14. What is the most used interest test?

   _____

15. What is research called which tries to determine if the situation causes changes in behavior?

   _____

# DISCUSSION

1. Have you ever taken a test which was considered a personality inventory? Discuss the pros and cons of taking such tests. When do you think these tests should be administered? Should the test-taker be informed of the test results? Why or why not?

2. When do you think projective tests should be used? How reliable do you consider projective tests? How are these tests interpreted, and by whom? Of what use may these tests be?

3. What is the basis for aptitude tests? When should they be used? How dependable are they?

4. What is the purpose of achievement tests? How are these tests used?

5. What is your opinion of the effectiveness of the Scholastic Assessment Test? For what is it used? Do you agree with this? Why or why not?

6. Explain how vocational interest tests are used. Why would several occupations which seem so different be clustered together on some of these test results?

7. How does the halo effect work in interviewing?

8. What is meant by the reverse halo effect?

9. How do you think standoutishness may affect a person's job performance?

10. Discuss the ethics involved in testing.

## ACTIVITIES

1. Many high schools administer interest tests to the seniors, and sometimes to juniors. Check with a counselor to see what tests are given and when. If you have already taken this test, perhaps you have questions about the results. Check with your counselor.

2. Research some of the different kinds of tests mentioned in the chapter. Discuss the pros and cons of each. Be sure to include the opinion you formed after your research.

3. Make a set of inkblots and show them to your classmates, asking them to write down what they see. Compare the responses of the girls with the responses of the boys. What differences, if any, were there? How did your own results compare with what the class saw?

4. Check your old copies of *Reader's Digest, Seventeen,* or other magazines likely to have tests on personality, adjustment, dating, etc. Take the test offered and score it according to directions. Then check to see how the test was normed. Did the article explain the validity and reliability of the test? How valid do you consider the test?

5. Write down a list of your aptitudes and interests. Have a parent or a very good friend help you decide those areas in which you excel. Decide how you would present each one if you were going to be interviewed for a job. If you are looking for a job, perhaps this will help you find one sooner.

6. Rate yourself on the scale below. A one or two means you have more of the trait on the left of the scale, a three, a mixture of the two. Four or five means you have more of the trait on the right. Have someone you know well rate you on the same scale. How do the two compare? Are these traits pretty descriptive of you? What others can you add?

| | | | | | | |
|---|---|---|---|---|---|---|
| adventurous | 1 | 2 | 3 | 4 | 5 | cautious |
| aggressive | 1 | 2 | 3 | 4 | 5 | passive |
| obedient | 1 | 2 | 3 | 4 | 5 | defiant |
| independent | 1 | 2 | 3 | 4 | 5 | dependent |
| bold | 1 | 2 | 3 | 4 | 5 | careful |
| serious | 1 | 2 | 3 | 4 | 5 | fun-loving |
| energetic | 1 | 2 | 3 | 4 | 5 | low-keyed |
| domineering | 1 | 2 | 3 | 4 | 5 | supportive |
| noisy | 1 | 2 | 3 | 4 | 5 | quiet |
| friendly | 1 | 2 | 3 | 4 | 5 | reserved |
| quick-witted | 1 | 2 | 3 | 4 | 5 | thoughtful |
| easy-going | 1 | 2 | 3 | 4 | 5 | moody |
| anxious | 1 | 2 | 3 | 4 | 5 | relaxed |
| impulsive | 1 | 2 | 3 | 4 | 5 | deliberate |

# Chapter 16

## Frustration, Conflict, Stress, and Drugs

## VOCABULARY

**A. DIRECTIONS:** Fill in the blank space with the letter of the correct term.

a. frustration
b. conflict
c. approach-approach conflict
d. approach-avoidance conflict
e. avoidance-avoidance conflict
f. double approach-avoidance conflict
g. anxiety
h. stress
i. distress
j. eustress
k. fight or flight reaction
l. adrenal glands
m. stress hormone
n. type A personality
o. type B personality

p. general adaptation syndrome
q. substance abuse
r. substance dependence
s. alcohol withdrawal delirium
t. hallucinations
u. psychedelic drug
v. synergistic effect
w. tolerance
x. paranoia
y. psychological dependence
z. opiates
aa. physical dependence
bb. hallucinogen
cc. steroids

_____ 1. A drug that distorts or confuses the user's perception of the world

___b___ 2. A problem that demands a choice between alternatives

_____ 3. Delirium that can result from severe alcoholism; includes weakness, anxiety, cramps, and hallucinations

___l___ 4. Glands that cause excitement in order to prepare the body for an emergency

___g___ 5. The feeling that something is wrong and disaster is imminent

_____ 6. Sedatives; drugs that reduce body functioning

_____ 7. Personality type associated with people who are always operating at full speed, are impatient, and are filled with distress

___e___ 8. A conflict involving a choice between two unattractive alternatives

___i___ 9. Stress that is nonproductive and that causes physical problems

___j___ 10. Stress that motivates us to do something worthwhile

_____ 11. Seeing or hearing things that are not physically present

_____ 12. The belief that others are out to get you

_____ 13. Artificially produced male sex hormones

___a___ 14. Process by which we are blocked or hindered from reaching goals _____d_____ 15. A conflict involving a choice between alternatives, both of which have good and bad parts

_____M_____ 16. A special chemical that signals the adrenal glands to activate or energize the body

_____ 17. Effect when two drugs are taken in combination, each is more potent than it would be if it were taken by itself

_____ 18. A craving of the psyche for a drug

_____ 19. A craving of the body for a drug

_____c_____ 20. Conflict involving a choice between two attractive alternatives

_____ 21. The physical strain that results from demands or changes in the environment

_____ 22. Personality type associated with people who are open to change, are flexible, enjoy life, and have low levels of stress

_____ 23. Use of a drug to the extent that relationships or occupational demands suffer

_____ 24. In relation to drug use, the body's adaptation to increasing dosages, larger and larger dosages are needed to get the effect produced by the original dosage.

_____ 25. A drug that produces major hallucinations

_____ 26. Abuse of a drug; the abuser has physical symptoms when the drug is not used; uses more and more of the drug

_____f_____ 27. A conflict involving a situation with both good and bad features

_____L_____ 28. The body's reaction to a crisis; the organism is mobilized to either fight or run away

_____P_____ 29. Sequence of behavior that occurs in reaction to prolonged stress; it is divided into three stages

## B. DIRECTIONS: Define the following:

1. defense mechanisms

_____

2. repression

_____

3. denial

_____

4. displacement

_____

5. reaction formation

_____

6. intellectualization

_____

7. identification with the aggressor

_____

8. regression

_____

9. projection

_____

10. sublimation

_____

11. rationalization

_____

12. self-concepts

_____

13. self-esteem

_____

# REVIEW/TEST PREPARATION

**MULTIPLE CHOICE:** Write the letter of the correct answer in the space provided.

_____ 1. Conflicts present problems demanding decisions. Which of the following is correct?
a. Once the decision is made, the conflict is solved.
b. A decision does not necessarily solve the problem.
c. If we make no decision the conflict will go away.
d. Someone else should make the decision.

_____ 2. An example of eustress, or "good" stress is
a. being called to the principal's office.
b. meeting someone new whom you immediately like.
c. taking a test for which you are unprepared.
d. giving a wrong answer in class discussion.

_____ 3. Researchers who deliberately frustrated people in a study found that those who were allowed to "get back" at the experimenters verbally, not physically, showed more release of stress than those who were denied this opportunity. This could mean
a. we should all fight back violently.
b. there are constructive ways to release emotional tensions.
c. we should never strive to get back at anyone.
d. some people have less stress than others.

_____ 4. Which of the following is NOT one of the stages in the general adaptation syndrome?
a. resistance
b. exhaustion
c. alarm
d. reinforcement

_____ 5. Major factors in the abuse of drugs are
a. peers, parents, and siblings.
b. school, work, and recreation.
c. stress, conflict, and frustration.
d. age, social status, and race.

_____ 6. Which of the following is an indication of alcoholism?
a. blackouts
b. morning drinking
c. going to school or work drunk
d. all of the above

_____ 7. A proven factor which causes a person to become an alcoholic is
a. genetics.
b. gender.
c. peer pressure.
d. none of the above.

_____ 8. Three categories of drugs are
   a. psychological, physical, and permanent.
   b. stimulants, depressants, and energizers.
   c. psychedelics, stimulants, and depressants.
   d. delusional, depressant, and dependent.

_____ 9. The process of explaining away a problem so that we don't have to accept the blame is
   a. sublimation.
   b. projection.
   c. rationalization.
   d. regression.

_____ 10. The image we have of ourselves is
   a. self-concept.
   b. self-esteem.
   c. self-contempt.
   d. self-descriptive.

_____ 11. Psychological distortions we use to remain psychologically stable are
   a. defense arguments.
   b. defense moves.
   c. defense tactics.
   d. defensive mechanisms.

_____ 12. The process of refusing to admit that there is a problem is
   a. regression.
   b. displacement.
   c. denial.
   d. repression.

_____ 13. The process of renting our feelings on something or someone other than the true or original target is called
   a. repression.
   b. displacement.
   c. projection.
   d. denial.

# WORKSHEET

**DIRECTIONS:** Unscramble the words on the left and then arrange the numbered letters to form solutions to the following:

**(a) C  U  R  T  S**

__  ‾2‾  ‾3‾  ‾4‾  5

The feeling which results when one experiences a set back, such as delay at a traffic light when running late

**S  H  E  R  F**

‾1‾  ‾6‾  __  __  __

**V  A  N  E  R**

__  ‾7‾  __  __

‾1‾  ‾2‾  ‾3‾  ‾4‾  ‾5‾  ‾6‾  ‾7‾  ‾8‾  ‾9‾  ‾10‾  ‾11‾

**T  I  N  N  O  E**

‾9‾  ‾11‾  ‾8‾  ‾10‾  __  __


**(b) K  L  I  F  C**

‾4‾  ‾5‾  __  __  __

Four alternatives which present problems for a person who is confronted with them

**N  O  A  C  E**

‾2‾  ‾1‾  __  ‾3‾

**C  R  I  L  E  C**

‾1‾  ‾2‾  ‾3‾  ‾4‾  ‾5‾  ‾6‾  ‾7‾  ‾8‾  ‾9‾

‾7‾  ‾6‾  __  __  __  __

**N  E  S  T  O**

‾9‾  ‾8‾  __  __  __

**(c) C O F I E F**

A reaction when an organism is suddenly confronted with danger

—  —  —  —  —  —
   1  8  2

**G I T T H**

—  —  —  —  —
5  1  3  4  12

   —  —  —  —  —    —  —    —  —  —  —  —  —
   1  2  3  4  5   6  7   8  9  10  11  12  13

**A V O R L**

—  —  —  —  —
      9  6  7

**T H I K N G**

—  —  —  —  —  —
     10 11 12 13

**(d) T E A L E**

Dependence on a drug which is "all in the mind"

—  —  —  —  —
  13 12

**D O E P O L**

   —  —  —  —  —  —  —  —  —  —  —  —  —
   1  2  3  4  5  6  7  8  9  10 11 12 13

—  —  —  —  —  —
   8  6    7

**C H E P S Y**

—  —  —  —  —  —
1  2  3  4  5

**G O C I L**

—  —  —  —  —
     9 10 11

**(e)  C  H  A  R  E**

—  —  —  —  —
3  4

Pressure and strain resulting from too many demands, or drastic changes in, the environment

**R  E  T  T  E  S**

—  —  —  —  —  —
1  2

—  —  —  —  —  —
1  2  3  4  5  6

**V  E  A  S  H**

—  —  —  —
5

**E  S  A  U  P**

—  —  —  —  —
6


**(f)  D  R  E  N**

—  —  —  —
3  4  5

Effect which results when two chemicals with differing structures are ingested

**S  A  N  P  Y**

—  —  —  —  —
1  2

—  —  —  —  —  —  —  —  —  —  —
1  2  3  4  5  6  7  8  9  10  11

**T  R  I  G  S**

—  —  —  —  —
6     7  8  9

**G  I  N  I  C**

—  —  —  —  —
10  11

# DISCUSSION

1.  Frustration is a blocking or thwarting of goals we are seeking. Explain this definition and give some concrete examples of some of your frustrating experiences.

2.  Stress is pressure resulting from situations in the environment. Make a list of some things you consider to be most stressful for teenagers, and then discuss some ways you believe the stress could be handled.

3.  Stress builds up. That is, when we feel pressure from all sides and nothing is done to relieve it, we become more and more tense. Some people react violently when they are experiencing an overload of stress. There are constructive ways in which this tension may be released. Discuss several situations which may result in a great deal of stress, and then seek positive ways in which this tension may be released.

4.  Much research has been done on type A and type B personalities. Discuss both of these types, giving the major characteristics of each and possible outcomes which could result from having one or the other of these personality types.

5.  The general adaptation syndrome is a sequence of events in which an organism tries to adapt to stressful situations. Name the three stages of this syndrome and discuss what each means and how the organism reacts.

6.  Discuss some of the factors which may result in a person becoming an alcoholic.

7.  Explain how the chemical structure of the cell and drugs interact to produce results such as drunkenness, hallucinations, and misperception by the senses.

8.  Drugs are divided into several categories, depending on the results they produce. Name these categories and discuss each in terms of physical or psychological dependence and tolerance.

9.  Name the defense mechanisms and tell when and how you have used each of them. Which is the one you will not remember?

# ACTIVITIES

1. Frustration, conflict, and stress are so interrelated that they are almost inseparable. When we experience conflicts we may become frustrated and/or feel pressure from these stressful events. There are four types of conflict which may result in varying degrees of frustration and stress. Using the chart below, give a personal example of each of these, the consequences or alternate choices, and tell how you resolved each.

| CONFLICT | Consequences or Alternate choices | RESOLUTION |
|---|---|---|
| Approach-approach | | |
| Approach-avoidance | | |
| Avoidance-avoidance | | |
| Double approach-avoidance | | |

Name _____ Date _____ Period _____

2. Look at the Psychological Stressors for High School Students on page 471 in your text. Create your own list by adding events that have happened to you in the past year. use a number system to determine how many stress points you are experiencing. Compare the lists with the entire class and combine into one complete list.

| Rank | Life Event | Stress Points |
|------|-----------|---------------|
|      |           |               |

3. Alcoholism is a major problem in our modern society among both the adult and the teenage populations. Conduct research on this topic and write a comparative report to answer the following questions: What percentage of the adult population has this problem? What percentage of the teenage population has the problem? What are some major causes of adult alcoholism? Teenage alcoholism? What are some major factors regarding adult alcoholism? Teenage alcoholism (such as when and where drinking occurs most frequently, peer pressure, etc.)? How are adult alcoholics and teenage alcoholics treated for this problem? What organizations are available for counseling and/or treatment of adult and teenage alcoholics? Any social stigma attached to either? Several sources of information may be Alcoholics Anonymous and hot lines. (If there are Safe Places in your area, you may wish to check with some of them to see if any teenagers have come to them because of drinking—either their own or their parents.)

4. Drugs, drug abuse, and drug addiction provide a never ending source of conflict and controversy among families, friends, and schools. Ask your teacher if the class may debate the issue. Your resolution may be something like the following: "Resolved: Legalization of drugs will greatly reduce their appeal and result in much less use among teenagers."

# Chapter 17     *Mental Disorders*

●●●●●●●●●●●●●●●●●●●●●●●●●●●●●●●●●●●●●●●●●●●●

## VOCABULARY

**A. MATCHING:** Fill in the blank with the letter of the correct term.

| | | | |
|---|---|---|---|
| a. | anxiety disorders | l. | thought disorder |
| b. | anxiety | m. | serotonin |
| c. | phobic disorder | n. | hallucinating |
| d. | obsession | o. | delusion |
| e. | compulsion | p. | schizophrenia |
| f. | somatoform disorder | q. | word salad |
| g. | dissociative disorders | r. | clang associations |
| h. | selective forgetting | s. | psychotic episodes |
| i. | mood disorders | t. | dopamine |
| j. | psychosis | u. | personality disorder |
| k. | flight of ideas | | |

_____ 1. A type of anxiety disorder in which a person becomes disabled and overwhelmed by fear in the presence of certain objects or events

_____ 2. A belief in something that is clearly not true

_____ 3. Disorders involving people's emotional states; includes depression and mania

_____ 4. A confused state in which thoughts and speech go in all directions with no unifying idea

_____ 5. Seeing or hearing something that is not present

_____ 6. A severe mental disorder that may involve disorganized thought processes, hallucinations and delusions, and major problems with emotional responses

_____ 7. Periods of psychotic behavior; they can alternate with periods of relative coherence and calm

_____ 8. A serious distortion in the ability to think or speak in a lucid and coherent way

_____ 9. Disorders whose major symptom is anxiety

_____ 10. Anxiety disorder characterized by an endless preoccupation with a certain urge or thought

_____ 11. A condition in which psychological issues are expressed in bodily symptoms in the absence of any real physical problem

_____ 12. A brain chemical; it is present in excess in schizophrenics, which causes nerve cells to fire too rapidly and leads to confusion in thought and speech

_____ 13. Speech in which words are mixed incoherently

_____ 14. Rhythmic patterns associated with psychotic speech

_____ 15. A disorder in which a person has formed a peculiar or unpleasant personality

_____ 16. A generalized feeling of apprehension and pending disaster

_____ 17. Disorders in which memory of a part of one's life becomes disconnected from other parts; amnesia, fugue, and dissociative disorder are examples

_____ 18. A brain chemical; levels that are too high lead to mania; levels that are too low lead to depression

_____ 19. An anxiety disorder characterized by a symbolic, ritualized behavior that a person must keep acting out in order to avoid anxiety

_____ 20. Forgetting only things that are very traumatic

_____ 21. A psychosis involving disorganized thoughts and garbled speech, as well as hallucinations and delusions; the most serious mental disorder

**B. MULTIPLE CHOICE:** Write the letter of the correct answer in the space provided.

_____ 1. A type of anxiety disorder characterized by frequent and overwhelming attacks of anxiety that are not associated with specific objects or events.
   a. specific phobia
   b. phobic disorder
   c. panic disorder
   d. agoraphobia

_____ 2. An anxiety disorder characterized by both repetitive thoughts and ritualized behavior is known as
   a. conversion disorder.
   b. dissociative disorder.
   c. hypochondriasis.
   d. obsessive-compulsive.

_____ 3. A somatoform disorder characterized by excessive concern about one's health and exaggerating the seriousness of minor physical complaints.
   a. dissociative disorder
   b. hypochondriasis
   c. conversion disorder
   d. somatoform disorder

_____ 4. The fear of leaving a familiar environment, especially home.
   a. agoraphobia
   b. specific phobia
   c. phobic disorder
   d. panic disorder

_____ 5. A mood disorder involving moderate depression.
  a. dysthymic disorder
  b. mood disorders
  c. fugue
  d. mania

_____ 6. A mood disorder involving extreme agitation, restlessness, rapid speech, and trouble concentrating.
  a. dissociative identity
  b. mania
  c. bipolar disorder
  d. mood disorder

_____ 7. Type of schizophrenia marked by strong feelings of suspiciousness and persecution.
  a. catatonic schizophrenia
  b. manic schizophrenia
  c. paranoid schizophrenia
  d. undifferentiated schizophrenia

_____ 8. A personality disorder in which a person has formed a peculiar or unpleasant personality.
  a. antisocial personality disorder
  b. borderline personality disorder
  c. personality disorder
  d. sociopath

_____ 9. A personality disorder marked by unstable emotions and relationships, dependency, and manipulative, self-destructive behavior.
  a. personality disorder
  b. antisocial personality disorder
  c. sociopath
  d. borderline personality disorder

_____ 10. A childhood disorder characterized by inattention, distractibility, impulsivity, and/or excessive activity and restlessness.
  a. attention deficit/hyperactivity disorder
  b. echolalia disorder
  c. autistic disorder
  d. bipolar disorder

## REVIEW/TEST PREPARATION

**A. TRUE/FALSE:** Write **T** if the statement is true or **F** if the statement is false.

_____ 1. In the United States, there are about 5 million people hospitalized for mental disturbances.

_____ 2. There is something "abnormal" in all "normal" people.

_____ 3. Agoraphobia is the fear of leaving a familiar environment.

_____ 4. A dysthymic disorder is major depression.

_____ 5. Depressed people tend to have low levels of serotonin.

_____ 6. People displaying abnormal behavior are usually very flexible.

_____ 7. Anxiety is a generalized feeling of apprehension which includes many bodily upsets.

_____ 8. The person with a panic disorder suffers from frequent and overwhelming attacks of anxiety.

_____ 9. A phobic disorder is one in which the person has control over excessive fears.

_____ 10. A sociopath is in constant conflict with the law.

_____ 11. An example of obsessive behavior is a person preoccupied with an urge or thought.

_____ 12. A compulsion is ritualized behavior that the person repeatedly acts out.

_____ 13. Dissociative disorders are common, everyday occurrences.

_____ 14. Amnesia is a disorder wherein traumatic memories "disappear."

_____ 15. A person with conversion disorder fakes physical ailments.

_____ 16. World salad is speech in which words are mixed together incoherently.

**B. COMPLETION:** Write the missing word(s) in the blank.

1. Four major symptoms that can appear in psychotics are

 (a) _____

 (b) _____

 (c) _____

 (d) _____

2. Some typical symptoms of major depression are

   (a) _____

   (b) _____

   (c) _____

   (d) _____

   (e) _____

   (f) _____

3. The behavior termed mania involves

   (a) _____

   (b) _____

   (c) _____

   (d) _____

   (e) _____

4. A bipolar disorder is one which involves

   _____

5. Schizophrenia is the most serious of all mental disorders. Symptoms are

   _____

6. The schizophrenic's unusual behavior comes in cycles called

   _____

7. One explanation of the thought problems in schizophrenics may be the presence of an excessive amount of the chemical

   _____

8. One particular personality disorder which causes problems for society is the _____,

   _____ formerly called _____.

9. The major problem of one who has an antisocial personality disorder is

   _____

10. The fear of leaving a familiar environment, especially home, is called

   _____

# WORKSHEET

**Characterize the following disorders:**

1.  Anxiety disorders _____

    _____

    (a)  Panic disorder _____

    _____

    (b)  Phobic disorders _____

    _____

    (c)  Obsessions and compulsions _____

    _____

2.  Dissociative disorders _____

    _____

    (a)  amnesia _____

    _____

    (b)  fugue _____

    _____

**Characterize the following:**

3.  Mood disorders _____

    _____

    (a)  Dysthymic disorder _____

    _____

    (b)  Major depression _____

    _____

    (c)  Mania _____

    _____

    (d)  Bipolar disorder _____

    _____

4. Schizophrenia _____

_____

5. Personality disorders _____

_____

    (a) Antisocial personality disorder _____

    _____

    (b) Borderline personality disorder _____

    _____

# DISCUSSION

1.  It is difficult to define abnormal behavior. The text has set forth a three-part definition of those who do need help. Explain these three parts.

2.  Describe phobic disorders.

3.  Explain anxiety disorders and the three different types of these disorders. In what ways are these disorders "abnormal"?

4.  How may a person behave who is diagnosed as having obsessions? Compulsions?

5.  What are dissociative disorders? Explain two types of this disorder.

6.  A moderate mood disorder is dysthymic disorder. What are the symptoms of this disorder? How does it differ from major depression?

7.  Explain the four major symptoms of psychotic disorders.

8.  Differentiate between hallucinations and delusions.

9.  Major mood disorders are major depression, mania, and bipolar disorder. Describe and explain each.

10. Schizophrenia is one of the most serious mental disturbances. Explain this disorder, including how the three different types of schizophrenics differ from each other.

11. Explain what is meant by word salad and clang associations.

12. What are the effects of environmental factors on schizophrenia? How do chemical factors relate to schizophrenia?

13. Characterize the personality disorders. The one which causes the most serious problems for our society is the antisocial personality, formerly called the psychopath. Explain why this is such a serious problem.

14. After having studied this chapter on behavior disorders, compare what you have learned with the way mental illness is portrayed in the movies and on television.

15. What do you think may cause depression among teenagers?

16. Many myths have grown up around suicide and people who attempt suicide. Discuss the things you have heard and read about this subject, and then divide the list between those things which are known facts, and those which are considered myths.

17. Discuss any ways you have heard or read about which have to do with dealing with a person who is suicidal. Make separate lists, one entitled "Do's" and one "Don'ts" in dealing with suicides.

18. Do you know anyone who has suffered from a strong phobia? What was the situation involving the phobia? Was the person able to do anything about the situation?

19. Describe what characterizes a dissociative disorder.

20. Besides schizophrenia, in which other forms of mental illness may hallucinations occur?

# ACTIVITIES

1. Try to visit a mental hospital. Find out what kinds of disorders are treated in the facility. What type of treatment is available? Which disorder does the largest number of patients have? What is the prognosis for these people? How many will eventually be able to return to a fairly "normal" routine at home? How many will remain institutionalized?

2. Secure a copy of the *Diagnostic and Statistical Manual of Mental Disorders IV* from a mental health agency, the local library, or from the American Psychiatric Association, 1400 K Street N.W., Washington, D. C. 20005. According to this classification system, there are ten major categories of mental disorders. List and characterize each. Present a report to the class.

3. Use of some drugs causes the person under the influence of the drug to behave in a manner which simulates certain forms of mental illness. An example is PCP. Do some research on how drug use may affect users and compare this with the mental disorders. Write a report on your findings and comparisons.

4. "Not guilty by reason of insanity" is a plea in court cases which has received much publicity, both good and bad. Research this, especially more prominent ones such as Sirhan B. Sirhan, who assassinated Robert Kennedy, and John Hinkley, who attempted to assassinate President Reagan. Are the people who used this plea still in mental hospitals? Do the symptoms presented appear to be those of genuine mental illness? What is your opinion of this plea, and why do you believe as you do? What is the exact meaning of this plea, and what happens to one who successfully uses it?

5. From the information presented in the text on what constitutes abnormal behavior, write what you think constitutes normal behavior. For instance, in the more severe forms of mental illness, the person is out of touch with reality. Therefore, it would appear that a mentally healthy person would have a good perception of reality. What about one's view of the self? What about interpersonal relationships? Is the mentally healthy person productive? How well does he or she know himself?

6. Watch several television shows which involve some form of mental illness and compare the way it is presented with what you have learned from the text. How accurately are the mental illnesses presented? What errors did you detect?

7. Because the media sensationalism about suicide tends to present a distorted picture, many people have misconceptions regarding suicide and people who commit suicide. Conduct your own research, using materials in your school and public libraries, talking with people who work with suicide hot-line services, and any counseling agencies in your community who deal with this problem, and write a report or make an oral presentation to the class which will present a more accurate picture of suicide and the people who commit, or attempt, suicide.

# Chapter 18    Treatment and Therapy

• • • • • • • • • • • • • • • • • • • • • • • • • • • • • • • • • • • • • • • • •

---

## VOCABULARY

---

**DIRECTIONS:** Fill in the blank with the letter of the correct term.

a. counseling psychologists
b. clinical psychologists
c. psychiatrists
d. psychiatric social workers
e. psychiatric nurses
f. psychotherapies
g. psychoanalysis
h. free association
i. transference
j. humanistic therapies
k. person-centered therapy
l. unconditional positive regard
m. behavioral therapy

n. cognitive behavior therapy
o. nondirective therapy
p. systematic desensitization
q. aversive conditioning
r. token economy
s. rational-emotive therapy
t. internalized sentences
u. awfulize
v. group therapy
w. encounter groups
x. electroconvulsive therapy
y. psychosurgery
z. irrational ideas

_____ 1. Broad term for any method used to try to help people with emotional and psychological problems

_____ 2. The process in which a person transfers emotional conflicts of earlier years onto therapist

_____ 3. A behavioral technique in which rewards for desired acts are accumulated through tokens, which represent a form of money

_____ 4. Therapy groups in which people are forced to share their inner conflicts and emotions

_____ 5. Therapy in which thoughts are used to control emotions and behaviors

_____ 6. Medical doctors with special training in mental disorders

_____ 7. Person-centered therapy

_____ 8. The process of saying whatever comes to mind; thought to uncover the unconscious in psychoanalysis

_____ 9. Albert Ellis' form of cognitive behavioral therapy; aimed at getting emotions under control by using reason

_____ 10. Therapy in which an electrical shock is sent through the brain to try to reduce symptoms of mental disturbance

---

_____ 11. Ideas that do not hold up when challenged by careful logic

_____ 12. Psychologists who deal mostly with problems not fitting formal classifications of mental disturbance

_____ 13. To see things in the worst possible light; Ellis' term

_____ 14. A behavioral technique in which unpleasantness is associated with acts that are to be avoided

_____ 15. Psychologists who deal with emotional problems of any kind; including those fitting into formal mental disturbances

_____ 16. Surgery that destroys part of the brain to make the patient calmer, freer of symptoms

_____ 17. The opinion we form of ourselves by listening to our own inner voices; Ellis' term

_____ 18. Therapies that emphasize the individual's ability to heal him or herself with some assistance

_____ 19. Therapy that uses principles of learning to alter the person's actions or behavior

_____ 20. Registered nurses with special education in psychiatric medicine

_____ 21. A behavioral technique in which the therapist increases the person's anxiety and counters it with relaxation in a graduated sequence

_____ 22. Mental health workers with a degree in social work; help patients and families deal with problems

_____ 23. Carl Rogers's humanistic approach; reflects the belief that the person and therapist are partners in his or her therapy

_____ 24. Therapy practiced by followers of Freud who analyze the psyche via the unconscious

_____ 25. A principle of humanistic therapy in which the person's feelings and thoughts are accepted for whatever they are

_____ 26. Therapy in which more than one person at a time is treated

Name _____ Date _____ Period _____

---

# REVIEW/TEST PREPARATION

---

**COMPLETION:** Write the missing word(s) in the blank.

1. The person who set mental patients free of their chains, and who began more humane treatment of the mentally ill was _____.

2. Differentiate between:

   psychologist _____

   _____

   psychiatrist _____

   _____

3. One who has a degree in social work and helps patients and families deal with problems is a _____.

4. A registered nurse with special education in psychiatric medicine is a _____ _____.

5. Methods used to help people with emotional and psychological problems are _____.

6. Professionals who try to help people with emotional and psychological problems are _____.

7. A form of treatment based on Freud's theory is called _____.

8. One technique used to uncover material in the unconscious is _____.

9. A patient who transfers emotional conflicts onto the therapist is using _____.

10. Therapies which emphasize the individual's ability to heal himself or herself with some assistance are called _____.

11. A form of humanistic therapy in which the therapist and the client are partners working toward a common goal is _____.

12. The form of therapy wherein the therapist and client are co-workers is closely associated with psychologist _____.

---

13. Another name for person-centered therapy is _____.

14. One critical thing which the therapist provides in this form of humanistic therapy is

_____.

15. A technique of therapy that uses the principles of learning to alter the person's actions or

behavior is _____.

16. The method in which the therapist increases anxiety and counters it with relaxation in a

graduated sequence is _____.

17. When alcoholics are given medicine to induce nausea and vomiting when they drink, the

method is called _____.

18. The form of therapy which combines behaviors and cognitions was developed by

_____.

19. The form of therapy which focuses on getting emotions under control by using reason is

called _____.

20. Therapy groups in which people are forced to share their inner conflicts and emotions is

called _____.

21. A controversial form of therapy which uses electric shock is _____.

22. A technique to alter the brain and change one's psychological state is _____.

23. A form of therapy which treats more than one person at a time is _____.

24. The opinions we form of ourselves by listening to our own inner voices is

_____.

## WORKSHEET

Complete the following charts.

| Occupation | Training | Task |
|---|---|---|
| Clinical Psychologist | | |
| Counseling Psychologist | | |
| Psychiatrist | | |
| Psychoanalyst | | |
| Psychiatric Nurse | | |
| Psychiatric Social Worker | | |

| Therapy | Method | Result |
|---|---|---|
| Electroconvulsive Therapy | | |
| Drug Therapy | | |
| Psychosurgery | | |

# DISCUSSION

1. Trace the development of our change in attitude toward the mentally ill.

2. What are the major differences between psychologists and psychiatrists?

3. Personality theory is important in treatment. Why?

4. Name and describe the three types of therapy most frequently used.

5. Differentiate between directive and nondirective therapy.

6. Transference means that the patient transfers emotional conflicts of earlier years onto the therapist. How may this be done? What are some conflicts which may be transferred onto the therapist?

7. What is the underlying assumption of humanistic therapists? What are their goals? How do they go about accomplishing their goals?

8. Explain how a behavior therapist seeks to change a person through the use of the principles of learning. Give examples and explain how the therapist may work to accomplish his goal of behavior change.

9. Think of a personal habit which you may wish to change. Explain in detail how this would be accomplished using systematic desensitization.

10. Aversive conditioning may be used with some alcoholics. How is this done? What other behaviors may also be responsive to this form of treatment?

11. What are the goals of the behaviorists? How do they seek to accomplish the goals?

12. How does group therapy differ from other forms of therapy? What are the purposes of group therapy? How do groups accomplish their goals?

13. What things do all therapies have in common, and how may patients benefit from therapy?

14. What factors tend to increase the effectiveness of therapy?

15. Three forms of therapy described in this chapter are drug therapy, electroconvulsive therapy, and psychosurgery. Explain each, and tell when and why each may be used.

Name _____ Date _____ Period _____

# ACTIVITIES

**A.** Opinions differ as to what is and what is not ethical in regard to treatment procedures. Who makes the decision about what behavior is right or wrong for the client or for the therapist? Whose well-being is more important, the person or society? Whose right is more important, the person or society?

After reading each of the following statements, carefully consider your response. Do not discuss the statement with anyone. Write yes or no beside each statement, according to your own opinion. If you believe the statement is ethical, write yes, if not ethical, write no.

_____ 1. Without giving his permission, Scott, an alcoholic, is committed to the alcoholic ward in a mental hospital.

_____ 2. Scott involuntarily undergoes treatment which involves receiving an electric shock each time he drinks alcohol, the result of which he learns to avoid drinking alcohol.

_____ 3. Jane has suicidal tendencies and in fact has attempted suicide several times. Her husband insists that she seek help from a clinical psychologist.

_____ 4. Therapists should be allowed to treat members of their own families.

_____ 5. A person sentenced to one year in jail has his sentence suspended by the judge on the condition that he undergo psychotherapy for the same period of time.

_____ 6. A psychiatrist has advised the judge to sentence a teenager to a psychiatric hospital. The teenager has murdered three people and has a history of violence. Treatment has been unsuccessful. The parents of the teenager give permission for psychosurgery. Three years later this teenager has had no recurrence of the violent behavior.

_____ 7. If a person with a personality disturbance is happy in this state and is nonviolent, should a therapist have the right to change this person's behavior?

_____ 8. Mental patients, without their knowledge, are used in determining the effectiveness of a new drug on behavior.

_____ 9. In order to lessen their sentences, inmates in a prison volunteer to participate in testing a drug believed to lessen violent behavior.

_____ 10. A teenager has consulted a counselor without parental permission. The counselor agrees with the request not to tell the parents the teenager is in therapy.

Name _____ Date _____ Period _____

**B.** Answer the following questions concerning the above statements and answers:

1. Which of the statements were easiest to answer?_____

   Why?_____

2. Which of the statements were hardest to answer?_____

   Why?_____

3. If the person gave permission, was it easier to answer yes?

   _____

   _____

4. If the results in the situation were good, was it easier to answer yes?

   _____

   _____

**C.** Now compare answers in the class and answer the following:

1. How many questions did you answer in the same way as did your classmates? Which questions?

   _____

   _____

2. How many of your answers differed from those of your classmates? Which ones?

   _____

   _____

3. On how many of the statements did the entire class agree?

   _____

   _____

4. How many other situations involving ethics in therapy can you list?

   _____

   _____

Chapter 19

## *Sociocultural Influences and Relationships*

## VOCABULARY

**DIRECTIONS:** Complete the crossword puzzle.

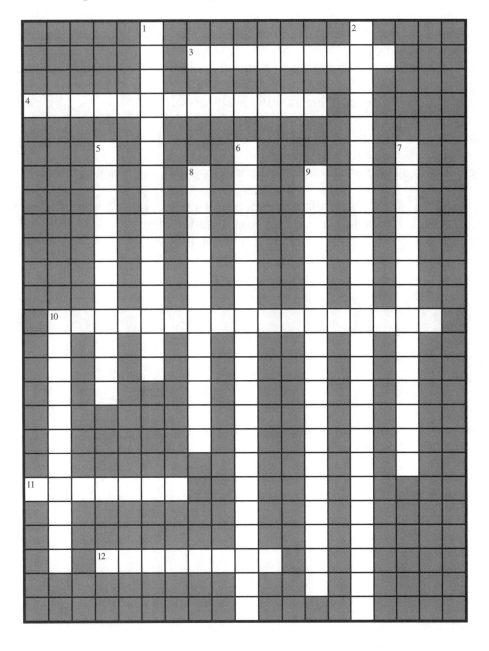

**ACROSS**
3. a supposed process in which a person gets rid of aggressive energy by viewing others acting aggressively
10. describes how people explain the causes of behavior. The process includes antecedents, attribution, and consequences.
11. a number of people per square foot in a given space
12. a psychological feeling of having too little space

**DOWN**
1. process in which a person loses his or her sense of individuality and responsibility as a result of being in a group
2. a process in which responsibility for helping others is spread out among the members of the group
4. an invisible bubble or portable area around each person
5. the act of making judgments about the causes for another's behavior
6. a situation in which the risk associated with an act is split among the members of a group; hence the risk is smaller for each person
7. an attachment to a fixed area designed as ours alone and the tendency to defend it against intruders
8. the emotional responses, behavior, and expectations that result from the attribution
9. process of learning behaviors by viewing and imitating others
10. information and beliefs a person already has about another

# REVIEW/TEST PREPARATION

**MULTIPLE CHOICE:** Write the letter of the correct answer in the space provided.

_____ 1. The three interacting parts of the attribution theory are
   a. affiliations, attribution, and consequences.
   b. antecedents, affiliations, and consequences.
   c. antecedents, attribution, and consequences.
   d. antecedents, attribution, and antipodes.

_____ 2. Both liking and love are based on
   a. mental awareness.
   b. familiarity.
   c. personality.
   d. emotions.

_____ 3. According to the text, it is most unwise to marry someone with these characteristics.
   a. excessive jealousy and violence
   b. stinginess and a bad sense of humor
   c. inferiority and clannishness
   d. unconcern and detachment

_____ 4. Evidence seems to suggest that aggression and violence are
   a. completely innate.
   b. often a result of imitation or social learning.
   c. the result of natural forces only.
   d. disappearing from the human race.

_____ 5. When people are ignored as individuals, this can lead to antisocial behavior. The term for this is
   a. depersonalization.
   b. depression.
   c. deprivation.
   d. deindividuation.

_____ 6. In the risky shift phenomenon, the risk or danger for each person is
   a. greater for the group leaders.
   b. the same for all group members.
   c. greater on group members than leaders.
   d. greater for the absent group members.

_____ 7. Because of the risky shift phenomenon, group behavior fosters more
   a. control.
   b. risk-taking.
   c. individuality.
   d. social awareness.

_____ 8. When one imitates the behaviors of others, it is called
  a. socialization.
  b. imitation learning.
  c. process learning.
  d. imitation programming.

_____ 9. Studies conducted on conditions under which people would help other people in difficulty showed that
  a. most people are uncaring.
  b. only certain personality types respond.
  c. the fewer people present, the more likely someone will respond.
  d. people do not feel responsible for the welfare of others.

_____ 10. The feeling which results from our concern about our behavior and what others think of us is called
  a. diffusion of responsibility.
  b. inferiority feelings.
  c. self-centeredness.
  d. evaluation apprehension.

_____ 11. The way we feel and the way we interact with others may be strongly influenced by
  a. personal appearance.
  b. the physical environment.
  c. relative attractiveness.
  d. the mood we are in.

_____ 12. Density is the actual number of
  a. people in an area.
  b. a crowd.
  c. people in and out of a room.
  d. people per square foot.

_____ 13. Crowding is the feeling of
  a. loneliness in a crowd.
  b. being trapped.
  c. being too close.
  d. pushing and shoving.

_____ 14. An attachment to a fixed area designated as ours alone is called
  a. territoriality.
  b. personal space.
  c. ownership.
  d. attribution.

_____ 15. The portable area around us that we try to keep from being invaded is called
  a. crowd apprehension.
  b. attributive space.
  c. territoriality.
  d. personal space.

# WORKSHEET

1. Define the three parts of the attribution theory:

   Antecedents _____

   _____

   Attribution _____

   _____

   Consequences _____

   _____

2. Explain the factors found in liking/loving:

| Factor | Liking | Loving |
|---|---|---|
| Physical Appearance | | |
| Familiarity | | |
| Interests | | |

3. Four very important tips from marriage counselors:

   (a) _____

   (b) _____

   (c) _____

   (d) _____

4.   Fill in the chart below on how the different factors may contribute to aggressive behavior.

| INFLUENCES ON AGGRESSIVE BEHAVIOR | |
| --- | --- |
| **Factor** | **Influence** |
| Cultural | |
| Social | |
| Biological | |
| Television and Movies | |

## DISCUSSION

1. The theory in this chapter which deals with our interpretation of the behavior of others is called the attribution theory, which has three parts. Choose a recent personal experience and apply this theory to explain it.

2. It has been said that "birds of a feather flock together," and "opposites attract." With which do you agree? Why?

3. Do you think it possible to love someone and not like that person? Explain.

4. Discuss falling in love. What is your own definition of love?

5. How important is physical attractiveness to love? Fully explain.

6. Is aggression learned or innate? Explain.

7. Explain the risky shift phenomenon in relation to aggressive behavior of a group.

8. How may biological factors affect aggressive behavior in an individual?

9. Much concern has been evidenced over the affect on people of aggressive behavior on television and in movies. Discuss the results of studies cited in this chapter of the text on this subject. What is your own opinion?

10. What is involved in offering to help someone?

11. What aspects of a situation determine whether or not help will be offered? The text discusses five conditions which influence whether or not someone will come to the aid of someone else. Discuss these.

12. Name and explain some environmental factors which may influence behavior.

13. Have you ever attended a concert where people seemed to be "packed" together? Explain your feelings and reactions.

14. Animals have a sense of territoriality, humans have personal space. Explain these concepts. One's personal space may vary from a few inches to several feet. Explain your own personal space with your boyfriend/girlfriend, family members, other relatives, friends, and acquaintances.

## ACTIVITIES

1.  Arrange with your teacher to have a member of the police force come to talk to the class about police experience with aggression and how it is handled. Ask for suggestions on how the class may handle their own aggressive feelings and how they may handle others' aggression directed toward them. If there is a prison near your school, you may also invite, at another time, someone from this institution to talk with the class on how aggression is handled there. Compare the points made by the two speakers.

2.  Have you ever been in an emergency situation and needed help? Explain the situation and the conditions under which help was forthcoming. Consider the findings of studies which were given in this chapter. Did any of the findings apply in your situation? Explain.

3.  Select one of the following situations and conduct an experiment on the willingness of others to help in a difficult situation.

    (a) Go to a shopping mall where there are pay phones, or find a pay phone in a place where there will likely be a number of people. Pretend you are making a long distance telephone call and need change. Ask someone nearby to get change for you, or to give you change.

    (b) Either in school or in a public place where there are a number of people, drop your notebook which you have filled with pages which will come out easily. Ask people passing by to help you. In school you may select a time when the halls are very crowded, and another time when the crowd may be smaller.

    (c) Go to a busy downtown street on which are located parking meters. Park beside a meter which has expired. Ask people who pass by for money for the meter.

Answer the following questions on each of the above situations which you used:

1.  How many people were present when help was requested?

2.  How many people responded?

3.  How many were present when help was offered?

4.  What were the reactions of those who did not respond?

5.  Were the people in what could be called a strange environment? How would this account for their refusal to help if such was the case?

6.  What factors may have caused people to respond in a negative way such as the way you were dressed, whether or not you were alone, etc.?

7.  What factors may have caused people to respond positively?

# Chapter 20

## Sociocultural Influences: Attitudes and Beliefs

## VOCABULARY

**DIRECTIONS:** Define the following terms:

1. internalize _____

_____

2. reference group _____

_____

3. stereotype _____

_____

4. prejudice _____

_____

5. illusory correlations _____

_____

6. scapegoating _____

_____

7. cognitive dissonance _____

_____

8. immunization _____

_____

9. discrimination _____

_____

10. sensory deprivation _____

_____

Name _____ Date _____ Period _____

11. culture _____

_____

12. ethnic group _____

_____

13. race _____

_____

14. attitude _____

_____

Name _____ Date _____ Period _____

# REVIEW/TEST PREPARATION

**COMPLETION:** Write the missing word(s) in the blank.

1. The groups to which we belong influence our attitudes. The more we identify with a group, the more we _____ its attitudes and beliefs.

2. The group with which one identifies and that provides a standard of behavior is called the _____.

3. A judgment of people based on the group they belong to rather than their individual characteristics is _____.

4. An _____ is seeing relationships between things that match previously held beliefs and ignoring what does not match these beliefs.

5. The odds of someone helping another across races is affected by whether the helping behavior is _____ or _____.

6. A _____ is someone on whom we place blame for what goes wrong.

7. One way in which attitudes may be changed is by _____ _____, or _____ _____.

8. We are in a state of _____ when our actions or events and beliefs are contradictory and cause discomfort so must be reconciled or justified.

9. Psychologist _____ pioneered studies in obedience to authority.

10. A two-sided argument in which opposing points of view are presented seems to be a good _____ against _____.

11. People who have important cultural and racial features, often including national origin, belong to the same _____.

12. Three factors which contribute to the brainwashing technique are _____, _____, and _____.

---

# WORKSHEET

---

**DIRECTIONS:** Unscramble the words on the left to find the solutions to the statements on the right.

**T    R    E    E    D**

1. Taking as part of ourselves the attitudes or beliefs of others

___ ___ ___ ___ ___
       3   4   5

**L    E    A    Z**

___ ___ ___ ___ ___ ___ ___ ___ ___ ___ ___
1  2  3  4  5  6  7  8  9  10  11

___ ___ ___ ___
10 11  7  8

**G    I    N    N    I    L**

___ ___ ___ ___ ___ ___
   1  2  9  6

**R    E    P    O    S**

2. A fixed set of beliefs about a person or group that may or may not be accurate

___ ___ ___ ___ ___
9  4  6  1  3

**R    O    S    T    Y**

___ ___ ___ ___ ___ ___ ___ ___ ___ ___
1  2  3  4  5  6  7  8  9  10

___ ___ ___ ___
   2      8

**P    E    S    T    E**

___ ___ ___ ___ ___
   7  5  10

**A    P    T    R    E**

3. Victim blamed for the problems of others

___ ___ ___ ___ ___
9  8  4  5

**L    O    G    A**

___ ___ ___ ___ ___ ___ ___ ___ ___
1  2  3  4  5  6  7  8  9

___ ___ ___ ___
6  7  3

---

**S C O R S**

$\overline{2}$ — — $\overline{1}$ —

**G U D E J**

$\overline{4}$ $\overline{5}$ $\overline{6}$ — $\overline{3}$

**T W E I R**

— $\overline{2}$ — — $\overline{9}$

**P I R E C**

$\overline{1}$ — $\overline{7}$ $\overline{8}$ —

**R E D E F O M**

$\overline{3}$ $\overline{5}$ $\overline{4}$ $\overline{6}$ — $\overline{12}$ —

**R E T C U R N**

$\overline{8}$ — $\overline{1}$ $\overline{11}$ $\overline{2}$ $\overline{7}$ —

**G R U P E**

$\overline{14}$ $\overline{13}$ — $\overline{10}$ $\overline{9}$

4. Treating people in a biased fashion, ignoring the real person involved

$\overline{1}$ $\quad \overline{2}$ $\quad \overline{3}$ $\quad \overline{4}$ $\quad \overline{5}$ $\quad \overline{6}$ $\quad \overline{7}$ $\quad \overline{8}$ $\quad \overline{9}$

5. A group with which one identifies and which provides standards of behavior

$\overline{1}$ $\quad \overline{2}$ $\quad \overline{3}$ $\quad \overline{4}$ $\quad \overline{5}$ $\quad \overline{6}$ $\quad \overline{7}$ $\quad \overline{8}$ $\quad \overline{9}$ $\qquad \overline{10}$ $\quad \overline{11}$ $\quad \overline{12}$ $\quad \overline{13}$ $\quad \overline{14}$

# DISCUSSION

1.  An attitude is a learned predisposition to respond in a certain way, either positively or negatively, toward other people, ideas, or situations. What attitudes do you have, and how did you form these attitudes? What are some major influences in the formation of attitudes?

2.  How can stereotyping affect a group and influence its behavior? What are some common stereotypes? Are stereotypes all bad? Why or why not?

3.  What is prejudice? What are some ways in which prejudice may be overcome or changed?

4.  Scapegoating may have some dire consequences, such as what happened in Germany prior to and through World War II. Exactly what is scapegoating, and how may it affect you?

5.  Attitudes are not resistant to change. How may they be changed?

6.  Have you had beliefs which were contradictory, which made you feel uncomfortable? This is known as cognitive dissonance. What can one do to alleviate this discomfort?

7.  Peer pressure, or pressure to conform to group norms, can be tremendous. In what ways does peer pressure influence you? What other groups exert influence on you? How? Were you more susceptible to peer pressure in junior high school or in high school? Why?

8.  Explain the results in the "learning experiment," and other similar experiments. Why do people appear to blindly obey authority?

9.  We are daily bombarded with persuasive arguments to do this, buy that, think this way or that, believe this. Explain how one may resist this barrage of propaganda.

10. Brainwashing is a technique that developed after World War II, and was used extensively in the Korean and Vietnam Wars. Explain why this technique proved to be successful. How may it apply to you as a consumer?

Name _____ Date _____ Period _____

## ACTIVITIES

A. Many of us are unsure of just what our attitude is toward certain subjects and issues. In order to help you clarify your own attitudes and beliefs, complete the following. Designate whether any change is the result of learning more about the subject, parental or peer pressure, maturity, or some other reason (state the reason).

1. Education. Attitude: _____

   _____

   Changed _____ Unchanged _____

   Reason for change _____

2. Nuclear energy. Attitude: _____

   _____

   Changed _____ Unchanged _____

   Reason for change _____

3. U. S. Foreign Policy. Attitude: _____

   _____

   Changed _____ Unchanged _____

   Reason for change _____

4. U. S. Domestic Policy. Attitude: _____

   _____

   Changed _____ Unchanged _____

   Reason for change _____

5. Capital punishment. Attitude: _____

   _____

   Changed _____ Unchanged _____

   Reason for change _____

6. Religion. Attitude: _____

   _____

   Changed _____  Unchanged _____

   Reason for change _____

7. Violence - TV and Movies. Attitude: _____

   _____

   Changed _____  Unchanged _____

   Reason for change _____

8. Pornography and Censorship. Attitude: _____

   _____

   Changed _____  Unchanged _____

   Reason for change _____

   List any others you may think of. _____

   _____

   _____

   _____

   _____

   _____

**B.** Write the common stereotype we hold for each of the occupations in the chart.

| Occupation | Stereotype |
|---|---|
| Housewife | |
| Teacher | |
| Student | |
| Principal | |
| Doctor | |
| Lawyer | |
| Secretary | |
| Electrician | |
| Movie Star | |
| Banker | |
| Policeman | |
| Plumber | |
| Judge | |
| Librarian | |
| Architect | |